£1·50

7

KHAO PHAT
FOR LUNCH

KHAO PHAT FOR LUNCH

LIZ CHALMERS

The Book Guild Ltd

First published in Great Britain in 2022 by
The Book Guild Ltd
Unit E2 Airfield Business Park,
Harrison Road, Market Harborough,
Leicestershire. LE16 7UL
Tel: 0116 2792299
www.bookguild.co.uk
Email: info@bookguild.co.uk
Twitter: @bookguild

Typeset in 11pt Adobe Garamond Pro

Printed and bound by CPI Group (UK) Ltd, Croydon, CR0 4YY

ISBN 978 1915122 346

British Library Cataloguing in Publication Data.
A catalogue record for this book is available from the British Library.

To my dad R.E.S. Chalmers, fondly remembered
for his support and encouragement.

Also to my husband Norman, for his
love, patience and fortitude.

THE HARD FACTS

When you become an expat within an organisation, you leave control of your life at the airport on departure from your mother country, because when you arrive at your destination, you have no idea what's in store for you.

Everyone has a different experience. Some companies are generous; others are not. Some give lots of information; others, like ours, prefer to let you find out for yourselves.

One thing becomes obvious: you are on your own, away from family and friends in whom you can confide (according to a poll conducted in Singapore, the one thing expat wives suffer from most is loneliness).

On the plus side you can experience another culture at someone else's expense.

However, the most important thing to take with you, besides your passport, is your sense of humour, because without it you will surely end up on the next flight home. But the first hurdle is getting there.

CHAPTER ONE

The Preparation

You could have told me I was going to the North Pole, and it would have been a relief – anywhere to get away from Birmingham. To be fair, several years prior to going there, we had been living in a cottage on a hillside outside Inverness and overlooking the Beauly Firth, with our nearest neighbours fields away in all directions. The past five years spent living cheek by jowl in the polluted, traffic-congested Midlands breathing in a cocktail of petrol fumes, whatever the local council used to spray the bushes and, of late, a fine dust said to have mysteriously made its way from the Sahara Desert, had not been a welcome experience.

A bread-and-water mortgage had resulted in me applying for a job as a lecturer at the local college. 'I only want a temporary posting,' I said. 'We've been told that we are only here for a couple of years, then we expect to be sent abroad.'

Thus, I made mistake number one: never believe what the company tells you. My naivety shone like a beacon. The wife of one of my husband's colleagues occasionally taught at the college and our conversations consisted of wondering where and when the next posting would be. Now, five years later, the news had finally come in the form of a phone call on my morning off. Thursday mornings were devoted to the washing, ironing, etc., part of being a wife, so the mention of the word Thailand had me agreeing to go before I realised I hadn't a clue where it was.

'So, when do we go?'

'W-e-e-ll, they want me there yesterday, but they've agreed to give me a couple of weeks to sort things out.'

'A couple of weeks! It's exam time, all that marking to do.'

'No need to panic. I'll have to go on ahead of you anyway. It'll give you plenty of time to sort things out over the summer holidays.' (Mistake number two.)

'Advised that you should bring a short-wave radio and that Oxo cubes are like gold', is all the information forthcoming by way of a memo from the other side of the world regarding our move to Thailand.

'I never use bloody Oxo cubes – is that all they can tell us?' My mouth is hanging open in disbelief. 'God, you'd think they'd give us a clue at least. How the hell are we supposed to know what to take? I thought they had been moving people all over the world for the past hundred years.' My other half, henceforth referred to as Mo, is, by this time, head down in overdrive mode, sifting through paperwork and filling in forms.

A trip to the head office in London is about as helpful as a day trip to Blackpool would have been as far as gleaning any further information is concerned. A charming girl in personnel produces an out-of-date copy (eight years, to be exact) of information about an apartment the company has long since ceased to lease in Bangkok. 'I'm afraid that's all the information I have, but I'm sure they'll have something worked out for you,' she says, adopting the reassuring tones of a British Airways pilot. The place we are going to is somewhere up-country, no one seems to know where exactly, with a name that defies any common pronunciation. I am beginning to have visions of having to trek through jungle to get there.

My place in the order of things had been clearly etched out earlier that morning by the doctor, who examined us and told me that there was no need for me to have a blood test, as it was my husband who was important as far as the job was concerned. In other words, they did not want to find out anything about me that might foul things up. They simply wanted him out there ASAP.

The extremely serious man from personnel who takes us to lunch says he does not know much about the place, but he believes a wooden annexe is attached to the local hotel. Images of a rickety wooden building set in amongst jungle territory flashes by and I jokingly ask if we would need machetes to get to it. He pauses, spoon halfway to his mouth, frowns, gives a limp smile, then carries on eating his strawberries, obviously not entirely sure and certainly not willing to commit himself. When asked how long we will be expected to be there, he informs us that the company would not send anyone to a place like that for more than two years. It is at this point a tiny seed of doubt begins to germinate in my mind.

When we leave the office later in the afternoon, neither of us is any the wiser other than we shall be entitled to an R&R once every month, which begs the question why and does nothing to bolster our confidence. The good news is that Mo has been assured that he will be able to go out and come back after a few weeks to finalise the move.

We do try to dig out as much information as we can ourselves, but everything seems to apply to Bangkok. The only place we find any mention of the town, whose name we can't pronounce, is in a reference book in the local library. Apparently, it has a beautiful Buddha but other than that it is not worth getting off the train. To make matters worse, Mo is so keyed up to go he does not seem to think any problem exists. After all, he keeps reminding me, 'I'll be coming back.'

A lady from the rental agency arrives to inspect the house. Mo's parents have come down for a few days to see him before he leaves.

His dad, dressed in a blue boiler suit, is busy tending to the flower beds. We invite the agency lady into the sitting room, which has large patio doors looking out onto the garden. She sweeps her eyes around, sits down on the sofa, declares this to be the best house on their books, and asks if will we be keeping on the gardener.

When I explain that the person doing the garden is my father-in-law, the poor woman is mortified.

Mo is still on a high two weeks later when he leaves to fly to Bangkok.

I get back from seeing him off at the airport in time to greet the man who has come to pick up Mo's Volvo, which has been sold back to the garage. The gardener I have found through an advert in the local rag arrives on his bike, camouflaged with an earthy patina that gives him the appearance of a newly risen zombie. Nicotine-crusted fingers clutching a cigarette, he proceeds to chain-smoke his way around the garden, viewed with great suspicion from a nearby fence post by our cat Hamish and me from the kitchen window. The man does an excellent job but can't fit in with my time off. I'm too nervous to give him a key; I'll just have to do the sodding garden myself.

The evening news announces that two convicts have escaped from the local prison. I do a double-check on all the doors and windows, thankful that Hamish is there to keep me company, but not for long, I realise with a sinking heart. The cat is the only regret I have about leaving. He sleeps beside me every night after that, which is a great comfort but only reinforces how much I shall miss him. The fact that he is going to stay with the family up north does nothing to alleviate the heartache I feel at having to leave him behind.

The next day I have a morning off. Boots have a sale on, and I spend an embarrassing hour skulking around getting funny looks from people as I pile up two baskets full of toiletries. I try to remain nonchalant as a year's supply of Tampax is blipped through and stashed into bags by a bemused assistant.

Next stop is a long chat with the bank manager re offshore accounts and more things than I want to remember. By the time I leave my brain hurts. That evening I must sit down and write out all this information for Mo before I forget it all.

Mo had said it was better that he left first as he would have a chance to get things organised and concentrate on settling into the job. Despite not being keen on this idea I must admit it does make a difference knowing that I have time to organise things at home over the holidays.

The blow comes when he phones. 'I need you out here as soon as possible. This guy is a computer buff, and everything is on the computer. I tried to explain that I knew nothing about computers, but he just said, "Don't worry, your wife knows something about them, so you'll be OK," and he left yesterday, so I really need you out here as soon as you can manage. Oh, and by the way, London got it wrong: the posting is for three years, not two, and I won't be allowed to come back after all.'

When the personnel lady in the London office calls to discuss the removal arrangements, the poor woman is subjected to a volley of my wrath and indignation, which her profuse apology does nothing to help.

Suddenly I find myself rushing around like a dervish and furiously writing letters cancelling our life as we have known it.

To make matters worse, by the time Mo had to leave, things had only been put into motion, leaving yours truly at the height of end-of-term exams and marking, to see the bank manager to arrange our yet-to-exist finances, dispose of my car, and find a new suite and a single bed for the third bedroom. I also must approve a tenant for our house, transport our beloved cat up to the family in Scotland, cancel the utilities and arrange for our worldly goods to be divided up into things to stay in the house, things to go into storage and things to go to Thailand. During all this frenetic activity I try to keep in contact with Mo, who, as far as ease of communication is concerned, might as well be on another planet.

'Well, I was hoping that this was all a bad dream, but now that you've phoned, I know it's for real,' I tell my friend Tess when she phones to invite me over for a buffet lunch with family and a couple of neighbours. 'This is turning into a nightmare; things are busy at work and now I have to organise this bloody move without Mo. I rang the agency this morning and they've just phoned back to say that someone wants to see the house tomorrow. I didn't expect anything to happen that quickly. The place is like a tip. But thanks, I'd love to come, it'll give me a chance to get away from it all for a few hours.'

'Great, have a large sherry and let me know if there's anything I can do.'

'Not unless you know someone who wants to buy a car. I've still got to get rid of mine and keep the frigging thing clean. You wouldn't believe the things that can't be done until the last minute; the paperwork is horrendous, all those lists,' I wail, unashamedly seeking as much sympathy as I can muster.

As I slop sherry into a glass I wonder how, on top of everything else, I can stop the garden from turning into a jungle.

It's amazing how comforting a sherry can be, I think later as, in a fit of reckless abandon, I sweep all the paperwork into the desk drawers.

My parents phone on return from holiday. They tell me that they have been talking to Mo's parents about coming to help me get the cat up to Scotland. The family is aware of my history with car journeys; something always manages to go wrong.

I also receive a letter from the RAC; they have misread our letter and prematurely cancelled our membership and cards. A hurried phone call is necessary to get the cards reinstated; the girl says she will try to see what she can do. I only hope the car doesn't break down, given my luck in that direction.

The removal men want a date and the furniture shop want to know when they can deliver the new bed and suite. I have managed to send letters off to the gas board, electricity board, water, rates and everyone else I can think of. The bank manager keeps asking for a list of standing orders. Everyone wants things now or yesterday. I am busy trying to book flights. The rental agency will have to see to new windows being installed.

I finally agree to rent the house to an Italian gentleman, at least I hope he is, who, hand on heart, assures me he will 'look after your ouse as if it were my own'.

This now means that the house no longer needs to be kept in showroom condition on the off-chance that someone might call. Nor do I have to restrict myself to certain rooms to save on cleaning or have quick, uncomplicated meals usually eaten before the food reaches the plate.

A letter finally arrives from Mo with a postcard showing the hotel. I am relieved to see that it looks to be a proper building, especially as our apartment is on the eleventh floor. The place sounds quite nice. I feel better now. He has sent a ticket for the trunk he had taken to a shop in Birmingham to have the lock fixed, but no map to show me where the shop is, so I waste an entire morning trying to find it.

On Sunday I drive to Tess's house for the buffet lunch. It's a beautiful, warm, sunny day and I am determined to forget everything for a few hours, simply relax and enjoy myself. The gathering is in full swing and Tess hands me a glass of white wine. I take a sip and savour the cool, crisp taste on my tongue. What bliss!

'I hear you're going abroad,' a voice says from behind me. For the next hour I stand with a polite fixed expression hiding my sinking heart as Ted and Myra from next door, spurned on by Bacchus, describe in lurid detail the pitfalls of renting, culminating in a horror story about someone in the village who had gone abroad and rented out their house only to have to leave their job and fly home six months later to try and claim it back. On my way home later, I think it is just my luck to have a sodding electric oven.

Unfortunately, my sudden announcement that I am leaving earlier than planned follows a television documentary about prostitution in Thailand. It leaves nothing to the imagination and of course everyone sees it, giving all my colleagues, especially the men, some embarrassing ammunition. I am hugely relieved not to be teaching on the 'legal secs' course, as it is lewdly referred to, and have to admit that my sudden decision to go does seem somewhat coincidental.

A few days later a black car draws up slowly outside our house in the early evening. A second dark-coloured car pulls up just behind it. I am sitting frantically trying to sort my way through the mounds of paperwork so hastily stuffed away in the euphoric aftermath of the double sherry. Our old office desk sits in front of the bay window, giving me a clear view of the comings and goings outside. I watch, fascinated, as two men emerge from the first car in dark suits and stare intently at the house. Something about them prompts an image of the Birmingham faction of the Mafia; they aren't big and broad, or even sleazy – in fact, one of them is quite good-looking – but when they start walking up the drive, I nearly wet myself until a third guy appears from the other car, and I realise it is Enrico, our prospective Italian tenant.

It has been a terrible week, the place is a mess and no way are these guys coming in. I keep them talking at the front door. They are very charming and so am I, even though I am inwardly seething because I didn't get a phone call first. 'No, I'm afraid you can't come in,' I tell my soon-to-be tenant, defying the pleading look and trying extremely hard to ignore his tall, dark and the most handsome of the three friends, who is busy taking stock of my entire body from head to foot with highly inviting liquid brown eyes.

Enrico's friends chuckle as I remind him sternly that he is expected to keep the garden tidy, which includes mowing it once a week, and tell them to make sure he does. I also have a quiet chuckle myself as I picture our stubborn, ancient lawnmower. It was bought second-hand and requires a ritual of much cursing and pulling on the starting handle to get it to acknowledge that it is still capable of coming to life. He has another go at asking for a gas cooker instead of our electric one, but I tell them my husband said no.

'If her husband says no that means no,' the good-looking friend says in a seductive tone that bears no argument. I swallow hard and say I have a lot of paperwork to do. They all solemnly shake my hand and go, much to my relief.

The elderly gentleman who comes every week to collect our football coupons and drop off the next week's supply says he is envious; would we like him to send the coupons out to us in batches of three or four?

It transpires that our foreign allowance isn't going to be paid into the bank as we thought. I have words with the guy in the salaries department; he apologises, but he doesn't have to face our bank manager. At this point I decide I am fed up with the company; I only hope the costs, of living out there makes it all worthwhile. I also discover that I cannot fax Mo in Thailand for some reason.

The bank manager who had seemed so understanding and eager when we first approached him is now more hesitant, as further in-depth discussion reveals us to be less prosperous than he thought. Having said it would not be a problem, he now refuses to give us a loan for the double-glazed windows that are about to be installed. I am in the reduced status of wife on her own with sinking funds. What a difference a man makes.

I leave the bank manager to go for my injections, delivered by an officious nurse who insists that my jabs are all out of date, so I need more than a booster. I also foolishly agree to a cholera injection and end up having two injections in one arm and one in the other. The result is I feel terrible that evening, as if I have flu.

I wake up next morning thinking I am OK, go downstairs to make some tea, suddenly feel sick and end up in a cold sweat kneeling on the floor. Somehow, I manage to crawl back upstairs and spend the rest of the day in bed feeling terrible, wishing I had never heard of Thailand and wondering how I am ever going to face the next lot of injections due before I must leave. Thank God it's Friday.

'You look terrible,' I am told when I struggle back to college on the Monday, my arms still feeling like lead weights.

'Oh, you poor thing,' a kindly colleague commiserates. 'When we went to live in Africa, we didn't bother having any injections – not even the kids, nor did we take malaria tablets and none of us ever got sick.'

I have already decided not to take the tablets. Hasty research has uncovered the fact that the tablets can make you go blind eventually, not to mention damaging the liver. My eyesight is bad enough already and the amount of alcohol I've consumed over the years has probably done more than enough damage to my liver as it is.

My nightmare reading is a book I have got from the library about rabies, not recommended perusing in bed for anyone bound for a country where rabies is rife. Nor does the small booklet from the centre for tropical diseases help to bolster my confidence. Instructions to wash lettuce in clean water and then dip it in boiling water for a few seconds are more than a tad worrying.

Meanwhile the removal company is pressing me for a final date, which means I must book my flight.

The evening news reveals that some psychopath is looking for women on their own on the motorway. A poor woman has been stabbed to death whilst phoning the police at an SOS box because her car had broken down. I decide that if my car breaks down, I will not move until a police car drives past. Next time we move we are going together.

When I am in the office the next day to collect something, a fax arrives via Singapore to ask for Mo's CV so he can get a work permit; it was urgent, they said. Mo is already working. The guy in charge merely shakes his head.

My stomach will not stop churning so I decide I need a couple of glasses of Sainsbury's Blanc de Blanc with my next meal.

My dear dad has opted to come down and help me drive up to Scotland. Unfortunately, he arrives on an earlier train than planned and I have gone off to college. Dad is tired after his journey and locked out of the house, so he spreads the paper he bought to read on the train on the front lawn and lies down to have a sleep, watched intently by Hamish. I am horrified when he tells me this later and hope the neighbours have not spotted him. The wall and hedge should have kept him hidden from view, but you never know. He just laughs and says it proves you should always buy a quality newspaper. A tabloid would not have covered the same ground.

A jerky trip round the local car park that evening reveals that Dad and my car are completely incompatible, so I will have to drive the whole way. Still, I am grateful for his company. We have dinner and then spend the rest of the evening pouring over the map, plotting the route. Next morning, after a few miles, I ask for a critical direction and discover Dad has packed the map in his bag, which is now lying on the back seat. True to form, I am so nervous that I take a wrong turning and must stop and retrieve the map. I am highly relieved when scrutiny reveals that we will not have to turn off the motorway until near Glasgow.

When we arrive at my brother's house, I discover that my niece's chic French penpal is staying for a couple of weeks. I don't think anyone notices my presence until I am about to leave a few days later. 'Oh, my goodness,' my sister-in-law says as we are saying our goodbyes, 'we won't see you again for a whole year.' I hope they remember that they now have the cat.

Mo's dad, of course, has seen the documentary about prostitution in Thailand and I am treated to an audio rerun, Mary Whitehouse fashion. 'Did you see what that woman had tattooed on her bare behind? "F Me", a word on each cheek and it was not just the F, it was the whole word, let me tell you! And they showed it on TV!' he says in a tone that implies that the fact that I am going there makes me somehow responsible for this disgusting spectacle.

Back home I am feeling awful and very much alone without Hamish. I drown my sorrows in the last of the sherry.

The removal men arrive a couple of days later. I have made all the necessary lists for insurance purposes and for the removal men, stating things to stay, things to go into storage, and things to go to Thailand; I have also labelled most of these things. When they start, I am horrified to find that, instead of doing one room at a time as I thought they would, each man takes off in a different direction, which means I must spend the whole day rushing up and down stairs to make sure nothing is packed that shouldn't be and that what is packed is going to the right destination. I only just manage to force a tight smile when one of the men helpfully points out that I am lucky I don't have kids to worry about.

When they finally go, I am completely exhausted. The house looks as though it has been burgled and someone from the agency is coming the next day to take an inventory. My dear colleagues have invited me out for a farewell meal. I somehow muster up the energy to go and end up thoroughly enjoying myself, which helps to take away the pain, at least for that evening.

During a cleaning blitz the next morning I get a phone call from the office to say that they had a fax message from Mo via Singapore. The list of things we had been told to buy in Thailand rather than ship out has been amended. I can now take whatever I like by way of crockery, glasses, kitchen equipment, etc.; in fact, most of the things that are now in storage or left in the house.

I fume my way into the front room, which has been our study, and realise that it was the original dining room and is now completely empty. We chose to put our dining-room table in the breakfast room. Now I shall have to buy another table and chairs. Shit.

Next day I check the local rag and spot an advert for a pine dining table and chairs, which I arrange to go and see. They are delivered flat-packed the next afternoon and the man kindly assembles them for me. Thank you, God.

My friend Tess and her husband Stu invite me for a final meal a couple of nights before I am due to fly to Bangkok. Tess is going to run me to the airport. She is a journalist and not one to miss a story. She announces, just as I am about to embark on my second glass of wine, that she and I are going to write about my leaving and a photographer will be at the airport to record the happy event.

On the fateful morning I arrive at the airport more tired than I can describe and discover that many of my dear colleagues are there to see me off. I say my goodbyes, dutifully pose in the rain at the entrance to the airport for the photographer, tickets aloft, and, too tired to shed a tear, leave my life as I have known it, for the last time. No one knows that I have packed the first seventy-five pages of a wannabe Mills & Boon-type romantic novel penned during the Easter holiday when Mo was doing a stint in Ireland and which I am determined will be my hobby from now on.

The Place

The Pits, as it is affectionately or otherwise known to the tiny expat community, none of whom can ever pronounce its name, is a busy provincial market town on the edge of the central plain. It is also in the hottest part of Thailand. Its most endearing feature is the muddy brown river, which acts as a parking lot for a plethora of houseboats, raft houses and, more importantly, restaurants. A complete dearth of any cultural entertainment or facilities in English means there is absolutely nothing to do socially (apart from going for a meal) other than drink.

Pits is not what you might call user-friendly for anyone who cannot speak Thai, especially if your mother tongue is English. Some English is spoken but rarely really understood and the difference in cultural approach to living means it is usually completely misunderstood.

A large part of this tiny expat community consists of people working for the oil company. There is extraordinarily little social interaction, we have been warned, and much depends upon the personalities of the people there at any given time.

It is a strange situation that we find ourselves in with Mo seconded to work for the weird hierarchy of living that exists in this microcosm of the oil company's world. He is with them but not of them, as they make it perfectly clear, which fits in with the chapter written by an oil company wife in a book about company wives that a friend gave me to read before we left.

It is to prove to be a strange relationship for both of us. We must be acknowledged, but nowhere in the rulebook or etiquette book do we come under any heading, so no one is ever quite sure whether to treat us as if we are below the salt or above it. Some of them deal with this by simply ignoring us altogether. Individually they will speak to us, on the whole, but if more than one of them is present it is obvious that they are uncomfortable, and it seems the best way for them to deal with this is simply to pretend we are not there.

They are not bad or horrible people, some of them are genuinely nice, some even become our friends, but they cannot help being obsessed with the expectations, dos and don'ts, and rules and regulations of this false world.

CHAPTER TWO

The attentive British Airways steward, obviously sensitive to my fear-of-flying vibes, plies me with enough champagne to knock out an elephant. Thus, he ensures that the ambient peace of business class is not shattered by a single female having hysterics when the pilot unnecessarily announces how many thousand feet we are cruising above ground level.

This flight that I have been dreading so much is blissfully uneventful but long and late, very late. To make matters worse I only realise that I have been standing at the wrong carousel when the baggage collection hall is empty, and my bags have still not come through.

Eventually I manage to retrieve my case and, with a reluctant trolley, trundle through a deserted customs area and out into the mêlée of Bangkok airport. My brain has not yet registered the fact that we have landed, and I feel as if I am in a surrealistic dream world as I walk the gauntlet of bodies straining against the barrier, arms waving signs with unfamiliar names. I search the faces for Mo and finally spot him ahead of me. Heaving a sigh of relief I beam him a smile, which is not returned.

'Where on earth have you been? Everyone else came through ages ago. I thought you'd missed the flight.'

Fit to weep, I chronicle my journey leading up to me standing in front of him. When I get to the part about waiting at the wrong carousel, he gives me one of his withering looks.

'I've had the company driver sitting outside for the past three hours,' he tells me, yanking my hand luggage off the trolley, whilst a strange man takes my suitcase.

'You could kiss me and say hello,' I suggest tightly, thinking that for two pins I could quite happily tell him to stuff his posting and get on the next flight home.

A terrible exhaustion accompanies jet lag, a pool of irritation sits in the mind, ready to erupt at any obstacle that delays the body finding a place to lie down and fall into a deep sleep. You only want to cut the crap and get to bed.

I get a perfunctory kiss with more grudge behind it than feeling. 'We have to hurry up; the car's needed back at the office.' And that is it.

I trail behind them thinking he should be more pleased to see me, until the first blast of heat from the Bangkok air hits me and suddenly, I am too spaced out to care.

In the car I feel vulnerable and involuntarily pull in my elbows as traffic whizzes past on both sides. One lorry roars past, too close for comfort, and I grab the seat. Mo stretches his hand across and covers mine. I glance up at him and get a softened smile. I smile back. *Everything is going to be OK,* I tell myself, *providing we survive this bloody car journey.*

'Don't get too used to this,' Mo warns me as I wrap myself in the luxury of long towelling dressing gown after a much-needed hot shower. 'This is the newest hotel in Bangkok. I booked it as a treat. We'll be slumming it after this.'

'Don't care,' I say, stretching my arms above my head. 'I'm just glad to be here.' Wrong move, I realise, as I am trapped by Mo's arms around my waist. We are both eyeing the bed longingly; difference is, I only want to sleep.

We have three days in bustling Bangkok before we must fly up-country to our destination. The next morning, I create a minor panic in the restaurant by asking for a boiled egg and wholemeal bread, which I quickly must amend to brown bread before anyone has a clue what I am talking about. After Mo has finished his breakfast, the waiter appears with a poached egg muttering something about *bow beh* and pointing to the kitchen. After much frowning and questioning on my part the waiter disappears again and finally arrives with a plate. '*Bow beh*, madame,' he says presenting two slices of brown bread. I grin triumphantly. Mo, now on his fourth cup of tea, lifts his eyes heavenwards.

The rest of the morning is spent in the office. 'This is Chantana.' Mo introduces the young Thai woman, who gets up from her desk to greet us.

'Welcome to Thailand.' Her face lights up with a beaming smile as she shakes my hand. I am also introduced to a shy young woman called Busaba sitting at another desk and a thin grey-haired man called Sunan who looks after the accounts. Chantana leads us to a door at the back of the room. 'Would you like some coffee?' she asks as she shows us into the spacious office.

'Hello. Welcome.' Mo's boss, M, comes forward to greet us with a broad smile. 'How are you?' He shakes my hand. He is a lovely, softly spoken Burmese man, who will, on many occasions, keep us sane and entertained over the course of the next few years. 'Please, take a seat.' He points to the small sofa and chairs across the room from his desk. He is delighted when I tell him that I want to learn to speak Thai. 'You have the right attitude,' he says. 'That is good.'

We chat for a while, and I tell him that I have brought the list of things to buy (all those things I could have had sent from the UK had I got the fax in time).

He glances at his watch. 'I must go now but Chantana will be able to tell you where to go to buy what you need; she knows more about these things than I do,' he says softly as we follow him through to the main office. A while later, after much discussion, we leave armed with all the necessary information re the various department stores and other places to try.

The rest of the day is spent shopping, with me learning how to pace myself, doing the 'Bangkok shuffle', as Mo calls it, walking slowly along the heat-laden, crowded streets and ducking in and out of air-conditioned buildings to cool down.

We shuffle along the main drag, Sukhumvit road. A wide expanse of five-lane highway roaring with a cacophony of traffic where the noise is earwax-curdling and the air clogged with fumes. The favoured mode of transport appears to be the motorbike and there seem to be hundreds of them. It is difficult to know which is the noisier, these or the miniature minibuses called tuk-tuks which I swear appear to rear off the ground when they accelerate, like bad-tempered Shetland ponies. Think of the noise racing cars make and multiply it several times. My ears hurt.

'What's that?' I ask, as a man peddling a three-wheel bicycle affair with a hooded carriage at the back big enough for two people, ambles up a *Soi* (side street) in front of us.

'It's a *samlor*,' Mo informs me. 'The quietest vehicle on the road, only here they are safer away from the main traffic.' The word literally means three-wheel, and the driver sports sculptured muscles in both arms and legs to prove how hard he must work to pedal one of these things.

We eventually arrive at a busy intersection, where we come across an enclosed shrine with beautiful Thai ladies dressed in authentic costumes, dancing to Thai music. This, Mo explains, is the Erawan Shrine, where people come to seek good luck or to ask for something important. Apparently, the owners of the Erawan hotel built the shrine, which honours the Hindu god Shiva, when some workers were injured in mysterious accidents. It seems that someone who asked for the god's help was rewarded by winning the lottery. Since then, a stream of people worship at the shrine, lighting joss sticks and asking for help for anything from business matters, winning the lottery, passing exams to having children. A courtyard has been built around the shrine, and to repay the god for wishes granted, people leave wooden elephants at the god's feet or hire the resident dance group to dance. This small courtyard is an unlikely haven amid the traffic chaos roaring past and around it. I make a mental note to visit it next time.

Over the next couple of days, we trail round the department stores pricing and finally ordering some of the things on the list, but they will not be delivered until the following week.

On the Saturday night we have a belated anniversary dinner with a bottle of wine to celebrate. The wine is so expensive it ends up being a joint present. At the end of the meal the waiter approaches the table bearing two silver pots aloft. 'You fuh coffee now?' he asks with a practised smile.

On the Sunday we laze around in the morning, braving the streets to take a short shuffle before lunch and then must leave two hours before our flight is due to allow for the infamous Bangkok traffic. The journey is fast but uneventful, apart from a panic-inducing moment when the taxi driver takes both hands off the wheel to '*wai*' as we whiz past a statue of Buddha. This is the Thai form of greeting and showing respect, placing both hands together as if in prayer.

We arrive at the airport too early and while away the time people-watching and commenting on the state of dress of the tourists. We count the number of 'wannabe macho men' for whom a vest and shorts teamed with flip-flops seems to be de rigueur, with no thought for the sensitivities of the country they are visiting. From now on, wherever we go in Thailand, we will not want to be considered tourists.

The flight is mercifully short and, as we come into land, Mo finally persuades me to look out of the window. Gripping his arm as if he has just asked me to dangle over a precipice, I lower my eyes and I am surprised to see that the landscape resembles a patchwork of muddy water. 'It's the rainy season and those are the rice paddies,' Mo explains. 'The monsoon rains come down like a waterfall when they start.' I sit back with a sigh and wonder if I should have packed my wellies.

As always, my whole body collapses with relief once we land and the awful roaring of the brakes has ceased. We shuffle out with our overstuffed hand baggage, smiling our thanks to the hostesses. The usual blast of hot air greets us and the heat from the sun licks the exposed parts of our bodies as we make our way across the tarmac towards the small airport building.

The place is chock-a-block with Thai people, many of whom I realise are staring at me. I look away, feeling distinctly uncomfortable. Foreigners are *farangs*, or *falangs*, for those who cannot pronounce the 'r', and I am acutely aware of being one.

'Good evening, boss.' A young lean Thai man, dressed in a white short-sleeved shirt and grey trousers, approaches Mo with his hands held together in the typical Thai greeting.

'Aroon, this is my wife.'

'Good evening, madame.' I notice he pronounces every syllable carefully as he greets me in the customary fashion and gives me a huge smile, for which I am extremely grateful.

I wait whilst they collect the luggage, feeling distinctly hot and sticky now, as well as strange, and very much out of place amongst the mêlée of jostling noisy Thai people around me. No such thing as a carousel here; the luggage is brought from the plane and dumped in an area in the corner.

Aroon goes on ahead of us and proudly holds the door open for me to get into the car. He has thoughtfully kept the engine running so that the air inside is cool, which helps stop me falling asleep.

I try hard to concentrate as we drive along the road. This is all so strange. We travel for a bit along the side of the rice paddy fields. I see what looks like a buffalo taking a dip in the ditch at the side of the road and we pass a few dirty cream-coloured bovine beauties, ribs sticking out but with eyelashes to die for, being herded along by a weather-beaten man wearing a large hat and carrying a long stick.

'Aroon is taking this route so that you can have a look at the town,' Mo explains as the scenery changes to houses in various shapes and forms, some seemingly abandoned halfway through construction. According to Mo this is because the owners ran out of money.

The car dodges through a mixture of traffic, ranging from bicycles, which seem to always carry two people, to tricycles with hooded seats behind them to carry passengers – 'Samlors,' Mo reminds me – noisy motorbikes, cars, vans, jeeps, the even noisier, smoke-belching tuk-tuks and large buses, all of which seem to propel along, kicking up a storm of dust, on the basis of every man for himself.

I count a family of five on the one motorbike, with a toddler in front of the father, one behind and the mother sitting side-saddle clutching a tiny baby. Another has two adults, two children and a dog hanging over the remaining space on the pillion seat. It appears that all the women prefer to sit in a precarious side-saddle fashion, seemingly oblivious to any danger. *This is all so different*, I think as I eye the passing buildings, rows of small shops. 'Shophouses,' Mo explains, when I comment on their size and the fact that they are stuffed so full that their wares spill onto the pavements.

'Did I just see a woman working a sewing machine outside that shop?'

Mo nods. 'You'll find there's sometimes hardly space to walk on what's jokingly called a pavement. Space is limited so they're used for everything.'

It's like watching a film; feeling strangely detached from it all, so unlike home. And then it hits me – this is home from now on. It will be another year before we visit the UK again.

The car draws into the side door of the hotel. A bellboy in blue uniform rushes out to gather up the luggage and put it onto a trolley. Once inside, I am pleasantly surprised. We walk across the marble floor to the desk, where I am introduced to Khun Pornsak, the manager. He is charming, has remarkably long eyelashes and tells me to let him know if I need anything.

'This is fine.' I force a smile, hiding my sinking heart as Mo shows me around the huge apartment. My first impression of what is to be home from now on is that, since the place has been empty for four days, someone could at least have vacuumed the carpet. It is a nondescript brown colour, speckled with bits of unidentifiable debris – nothing serious but enough to niggle.

The next thing that hits, as I follow Mo on a guided tour, is the sheer size of the place. It has been converted from no less than six hotel rooms, including en-suite bathrooms, one of which has been turned into a small kitchen, another a laundry and yet another a storeroom. It has three working bathrooms, two of which are en-suite in each of the bedrooms and one a quick hop across from the kitchen – custom-made for my weak bladder. The lounge/dining area is huge, having been three rooms knocked into one.

Mo has been living here for a week before I arrived and, having seen it first with all his predecessor's furniture in it, was sadly disappointed when it was left with only the skeleton combination of hotel and company furniture.

'I managed to persuade the hotel manager to give us some extra chairs and a small table,' he says, anxious for me to like the place.

'Mm.' I force a smile, mentally trying to make the blue-and-white-striped cushion covers on the cane chairs match the brown carpet and thankful that the room is big enough not to let it clash with the brown-and-cream-patterned company suite and hotel cane with yellow-top dining table. At least the suite matches the carpet, even if it turns out to be the most spine-torturing concoction we have ever sat on. Neither of us comments on the company teak-coloured units, nor the two hideous side tables that look as though they have ingrown feet.

I shiver in the unaccustomed coolness of the air-conditioned room. Jet lag has left me constantly fighting tiredness and irritability. 'It's fine, really.' I try to assure him and myself with another smile.

'Anyway, we can move if we want to.' I feel Mo hovering behind me as I open the doors leading onto the narrow balcony. The noise of the traffic is deafening. I look down and then flinch backwards, my fear of heights rushing through my body. God, it is a long way down. 'Let's have a shower and then we'll have something to eat,' Mo says, sensing my unease.

Later, showered and dressed, we make our way down to the coffee shop on the ground floor. The cane tables and chairs are set out on a terracotta floor, Spanish-style. The dimmed lights, low ceiling and dulcet tones of the resident would-be singers add an air of intimacy, whilst a table full of inebriated Thai men puffing and gesticulating with lighted cigarettes, supply the smoke.

The colour of the menu in this dimmed light, plus the fact that the print is set against a background picturing the local river and its riverboats, makes it almost impossible to read.

'It's easier to read during the day,' Mo says. 'Why don't we just eat Thai-style? I'll order a few dishes and then we can share them, OK?'

I nod, finding it all so strange, but a tinge of excitement is seeping through the jet lag. I am eager to experience this new culture and enjoy it. I can sense that Mo feels the same way. Although he is more widely travelled than I am, neither of us has experienced living in a different country for any length of time.

'Good evening, Khun Mo, good evening, madame.' The head waitress, an attractive young woman, greets us. *Khun* is used as a mark of respect towards both sexes. Everything said by a woman ends with *kha* and everything said by a man ends with *krap*, which I cannot help thinking is extremely appropriate and sums things up nicely.

Mo introduces me. Her name is Lalana. 'Your wife very bootiful,' she tells Mo. In my present state of dog-tiredness, I decide this woman will go far. She and Mo joke together, and when another waitress comes to the table and joins in, I decide Khun Mo probably has not had such a terrible time without me after all.

24

The food is different from anything I have ever tasted, especially the tom yum soup, which has bits in it that Mo informs me are not meant to be eaten, but it is delicious, and I decide there and then I will not be looking for any Western-style cooking for a long time.

'We'll eat in the hotel for the first week,' Mo says, much to my relief, 'just to give you a chance to find your way about, but you're going to have to get used to going to the market.' His eyes narrow ominously. 'Try walking around the one nearest the hotel first; you have to learn to pace yourself in this heat, just go a bit further each day.' He smiles encouragingly.

You do not get over jet lag quickly; it slowly seeps out of the system, lurking around for days, waiting to strike. It strikes now. I just want to go to sleep, but Mo insists I stay up. 'We'll go for a walk around outside for a bit; if you go to bed now, you'll only wake up at midnight or some ungodly time in the morning.'

It's pitch-black outside, apart from the lights shining from the hotel and all the busy shop fronts. Once I get over the initial welcoming blast of hot air, after the fierce coolness of the hotel air-conditioning system, I realise that the street is bustling with activity. All the tiny shops are open for business and lots of people are walking around or sitting huddled over plates, eating. The traffic seems not to have let up since earlier on and not every machine has the luxury of a headlight, so between that and trying to make sure you do not stumble over something sticking up in the dark, walking is quite precarious. Some peculiar smells are also wafting around.

We eventually manage to cross the road onto the narrow pavement that has been laid to include the trees and any other objects that might have been sticking up when the cement was put down. The first corner we come to gives home to a restaurant where a fiercely hot, long narrow barbeque sits on the pavement. Trying to get past this is a feat in itself, a case of risk burning yourself or being run over by the traffic on a horrendously busy road. The possibility of breaking your ankle and being bitten by a rabid dog cannot be dismissed either, as the pavement is unusually high, and a seriously mangy dog has chosen to go to sleep at the side of the road. It does not do to keep your eyes on your feet nor become too complacent. 'You have to watch out,' Mo warns me, ever-conscious of my habit of walking along in a daydream. 'The shop awnings hang at spurious heights, most often at eyebrow height and sometimes lower, so be careful.'

We have no iron, so that is the first thing on our list of things to buy, and after peering for ages into the dusty window of one of many small electrical shops, we finally spy a steam iron and pounce on it like a mirage that might disappear. It is covered in dust, but we don't care; it is the only one in town and we are having it. It soon becomes obvious that many of the items that we take for granted are not going to be found in Pits, so we resign ourselves to having to wait until our R&R in Bangkok.

I cannot get over how busy everything seems.

Mo shows me the small 'supermarket' store where I can buy milk and other necessities and then points out the narrow entrance into the market where all the fresh produce is sold. 'It smells a bit at first but if you keep going you get used to it. There's no such thing as a butcher's shop or a fish shop,' he warns me. 'You have to buy it all either in here or at one of the other markets.' Finally, I am too tired to care where I am, and we make our way back to the apartment.

Later, in the bathroom, I come across the biggest cockroach I have ever seen. It makes a run for it when I scream and ends up clinging to the back of the water glass. 'You'll have to come and do something about it,' I wail, being a total wimp when it comes to killing anything. Mo is decidedly put out, having just settled himself in bed. I watch anxiously as he pursues it around the bathroom, finally managing to whack it with the toilet brush and then flush it down the bowl. 'I hope it was dead,' I mumble, feeling part guilt and part fear that it might be able to resurrect itself and swim back up to get its revenge.

'Course it's bloody dead,' Mo retorts with a withering look on his way back to bed.

The next morning has us up bright and early as Mo starts work at 7.30am, which, for him, means waking up before mind and body are fully synchronised.

A 'bloody hell' from the bathroom is followed by Mo appearing with towel around his waist and grabbing the phone. 'There's no hot water,' he rages politely down the receiver. 'No hot water, you tell manager. I speak to manager. You tell him I speak to him later.' Receiver is crashed back down. I sigh and decide on a quick splash followed by a serious shower when the water has heated up.

'They don't have brown bread,' Mo warns me. On his advice I order scrambled egg, which they can do, but I am disappointed when it becomes obvious that the toast is thin, white, sliced bread. The coffee is not the freshly ground I was hoping for, but in the present climate it does not do to complain. We finish breakfast and then go back up to the apartment so that Mo can brush his teeth and collect his things. By this time, he seems in a better humour as we kiss goodbye.

I shower nervously under the now hot water, remembering the cockroach and hoping it does not have another half, intent on revenge. A knock at the door later reveals a maid dressed in a blue uniform consisting of a shirt-style top and culottes. She smiles. 'Good morning, madame. I clean?'

Her name is Kik, she tells me. I invite her in and try broaching the subject of a vacuum cleaner and then deeply regret even thinking about it, as it soon becomes clear this girl speaks truly little English and has not a clue what I am talking about. She watches my gyrations with a look of bemused puzzlement. 'Madame, I go,' she says, and disappears out of the door. *Oh God, she thinks I am mad.* I stand, a dejected failure in the middle of this vast room, hoping she will come back.

A few minutes later, I hear voices in the distance, which gradually become louder until the maid appears with another girl who seems older and self-assured. She is trailing a large machine behind her that looks like a stunted Dalek but which I take to be the vacuum cleaner. I am temporarily elated until they start the thing up and it seems that my first observation might have been correct. This is when I take over and with much gesticulating get them to take the top off so I can at least determine whether this tube of metal on wheels is man-made or indeed of the alien variety. Several clouds of dust later we discover that the filters, sadly, are clogged beyond redemption and I decide to give up and try another day. I am surplus to requirements, so I hastily gather up my handbag and leave them to it.

The lobby downstairs is virtually empty apart from some people sitting in a few of the basket weave armchairs set around coffee tables in the lounge area. I make my way across the marbled hall and open the door to be met with the familiar hot blast of air, a welcome comfort after the clinical coolness of the hotel AC. A surge of excitement races up my spine as I walk down the steps to the pavement. I am ready to tackle my first solo expedition, consciously trying to remember Mo's Bangkok shuffle and walk slowly, 'otherwise you'll tire yourself out in the heat'.

In the harsh light of day, I discover what a typical Asian town means by way of heat, dust and weird smells that I do not even like to guess at; so much was hidden in the velvet cloak of darkness the night before. It all seems much more real and threatening now, especially the traffic.

I stand on the edge of the pavement and wonder how on earth I am going to get across. Watching this cacophony of vehicles from the car was one thing but having to face it solo is something else. Not only is it noisy beyond belief, as motorbikes and angry-sounding tuk-tuks roar past, all jostling for position, but the fumes they spew out invite suicide by suffocation.

The prospect of trying to cross the road seems for the moment quite daunting, so I decide to make my way along the pavement in the hope that there will be a let-up along the way for long enough to allow me to cross safely. Unfortunately, after several yards and experiencing some very odd smells, the pavement ends abruptly. I am now faced with a line of parked *samlors*, their drivers' languid bodies splayed about like corpses after a machine-gun attack. A few of the drivers who are not asleep signal to me in the hope of getting a fare, their exposed flesh a weather-beaten nut brown.

'No, thanks.' I shake my head. I have enough problems to contend with trying to avoid the traffic, without making a conscious effort to join it. It soon becomes clear that they have neither such a thing as a highway code nor any concept of danger, as motorbikes weave in and around other forms of traffic with a complete disregard for anyone else. It is no more organised than dodgems at the fair ground.

This is awful, I decide, after several aborted attempts. *I am going to be here all bloody day at this rate.* I wonder if there is a traffic warden equivalent to Saint Anthony who Tess assures me will find anything for you; you only have to ask. *Oh please,* I beg silently in the hope that he might see his way to helping a lapsed Protestant just this once.

I think I might as well give up and then I see a large Doberman dog walking up to the edge of the pavement. I swear it looks both ways before it starts to cross. I wince and wait for the carnage, but no, as the first vehicle approaches, the trailblazer on paws stops, steps back slightly, head cowed, then starts again, repeating the process as the traffic begins to weave around it until finally it gets to the other side. I am so filled with admiration I nearly applaud it.

When a second Doberman arrives, I take this as a sign from above and decide my only bet is to follow in its wake. I cross my fingers, fervently hoping that the Buddhist aversion to killing animals will, at least on this occasion, stretch to humans as well.

I feel it is the equivalent to walking on water, when I reach the other side, still intact, and say a polite thank-you to the Doberman just in case I should require his services as a traffic warden again.

I soon begin to wonder why I bothered as I pick my way round yet another tree stump sticking up through the pavement and then narrowly avoid colliding with the knotted end of an electric cable, wires bared and dangling dangerously at eye level.

Just as I am gaining confidence, despite the weird, warm odours drifting up my nostrils, I discover that I must run the gauntlet of the barbeque on the corner. I consider my options carefully and then decide I have to breathe in and walk sideways to avoid being singed. Leaving the pavement is out of the question; it is a particularly busy traffic junction, and if I step down, I risk treading on the sleeping resident mangy dog, which does not appear to have moved from the night before.

I emerge from this tricky manoeuvre amazingly unscathed. Not a scorch mark in sight, I see as I quickly examine my clothes. Now I turn left to go down to the market and almost gag from the smell, I quickly fumble in my bag for a tissue, and with it firmly glued to my nose I look around and spot two of the filthiest children I have ever seen standing gaping at me from amidst a pile of rubbish on the other side of an open doorway.

I hold my breath and hurry on until I am well clear of this part of the pavement, and then I see the entrance to the marketplace on the other side of the street. The street market, which I was told starts in the early hours of the morning, is all miraculously cleared away by eight-thirty in the morning, but this covered market goes on all day.

The entrance is long and narrow and looks promising, flanked by ladies squatting comfortably on the ground, surrounded by huge round baskets brimming with vegetables and fruits. The ladies smile and I smile back. I almost fall in love with the place there and then, but as I walk further down, I become aware of a terrible smell. This must be what Mo was talking about last night.

By this time, the heat is oppressive, and already my bra is clamped to my body with sweat. At first, I am convinced something must have died and then I realise the smell is coming from the baskets filled with dried fish and the basins with huge mounds of some paste or other. I must admit the colours, which range from shades of rustic pinks and browns through to a deep, almost purple colour, would give inspiration to any autumn collection, but the smell I am sure would put even a hyena off its lunch.

I stop breathing for as long as I can and hurry on, more intent on escaping from the smell than where I am headed. The result is that I get myself completely lost. By this time, the sweat from my eyebrows is dripping into my eyes and making my mascara run. This forms a stinging cocktail, causing me to dab my eyes with a tissue, thereby threatening to dislodge a contact lens; my T-shirt is soaked and my bra feels like a vice.

I think I am going to die if I do not get out of here soon. Then I feel something brush against my hair and, when I turn round, I come face to face with what looks like a gaping pink hole. Just a few seconds later I realise that it is the severed end of a grinning pig's head swaying on the end of a hook. I get a hell of a fright and after that everywhere I turn there seem to be more grinning pigs' heads. One has a plastic flower stuck in its ear.

I hurry away and pass a guy kneeling in front of a pig's head, calmly shaving its face. The worst thing is the pig looks as if it is enjoying it! Now I am convinced this is a surrealistic nightmare and I desperately want to get out of it.

Round the corner I come across several fish splashing and slapping around in only an inch of water; one leaps out of the basin in front of me and proceeds to make a getaway. Then this woman picks up one of the fish in the basin and pins it down by its head. In the meantime, she calmly carries on her conversation as if she had just picked up a cucumber. I watch in horror as the poor fish is flapping away frantically while the woman pauses, mid conversation, waving the knife around to emphasise a point before she brings it down to take a chop at the poor fish. She stops again to wave the knife, laughing and chatting away to her friends, completely oblivious to the fact the fish is still alive and probably in agony. This carries on until the poor thing is merely a pile of fish steaks chucked into a plastic bag and handed over.

When I see someone else buying fish that are thrown live into the plastic bag, I decide that fish will not be on the menu.

Round yet another corner I come across a stall selling chickens. It is a relief when I see that the chickens are at least dead and cut up, then I hear a soft clucking noise. I really wish I had not looked. The poor things are lying underneath the stall with all their feet tied together. This is horrible and even worse when I watch a man pick them up and carry them away upside down in a bunch.

I am fast on my way to becoming a vegetarian. The next thing I see a few stalls down is a basin full of frogs. They are all crawling over each other, trapped underneath a net. Then I see another basin with pink frogs in it lying on their backs but still breathing. To begin with I think this is a new breed of frog until I watch a woman pick up one of the ordinary frogs; she slits it from head to foot and then peels its skin off.

At the next stall is a basin filled with enormous beetle-like insects crawling listlessly over a bed of leaves. These I do not even want to think about.

This really is a nightmare: there are flies everywhere, landing on raw pork, chicken, fish, then onto fresh noodles, vegetables, fruit, dog shit, whatever. Cats and flea-bitten, mangy dogs covered in sores run around freely, and I watch as one dog nonchalantly lifts its leg and pees into a basket of pineapples.

By the time I find my way out I feel sick, disillusioned and convinced I will never be able to produce a meal again, let alone stifle my imagination for long enough to eat it.

When I see Mo later, we do the banking, which is surprisingly easy, and then go for lunch. 'You should have used something as a landmark,' Mo is busy telling me as we make our way back to the car.

'I did, at least I thought I had, but one pig's head looks much the same as any other,' I tell him as I pick my way past a couple of men squatting on the pavement, weighing out spices. I then neatly avoid tripping over what looks like a huge nail sticking out from the concrete.

A piece of material hanging at the side of the shop catches my eye. 'Just a minute,' I call to Mo and stop to have a look. When I start on my way again, I realise Mo has not heard me. *Damn, why is he always in such a rush?* I curse him silently, and hurry to catch up. Then I feel the sickening thud. It takes a few stunned seconds before I realise that I have just walked into an awning.

To make matters worse Mo has not noticed; in fact, no one has. I suddenly find myself hemmed in by the paraphernalia of shophouses on one side and traffic on the other in a strange, hot, dusty street, feeling momentarily stunned, stupid to have let it happen and with a head that hurts more than I can describe. The shock brings tears to my eyes, and I find myself having to seriously struggle with my emotions to stop myself from bursting into tears.

'How's the head?' Mo ventures to ask after we have ordered lunch: a chicken curry for him and a Thai soup for me, my appetite having dwindled, and not only because of my head.

'Throbbing a bit, but I'll live.' I force a tight smile. It is a relief to be back in the cool climate of the air-conditioned coffee shop, although I could do without the plaintiff voice of the singer reverberating in my ears. The volume of the microphone always seems to be unnecessarily high for the size of the place.

Mo's eyes visibly soften as he contemplates the lump I can feel emerging by the minute on my forehead. 'You have to be careful of those awnings. There aren't any laws here about what height they are supposed to be.'

'I just got such a shock.' The memory of the explosion in my head when it met the iron awning bar at fast walking speed is still vivid in my mind. 'I was hurrying to catch up with you,' I say accusingly.

'Oh, so it's my fault.' He lets out a soft, incredulous laugh.

'Well, it never seems to occur to you that I might actually want to look at things. You always charge on ahead,' I counter defiantly.

'We had to get back to have lunch. I haven't got all day to do as I please,' he says pointedly. 'I've got work to do,' he adds, a tad angrily, I notice, and resent his attitude. 'You've just got to take things slowly and watch where you're going, that's all.'

At that point, the waitresses arrive with the food and set it down in front of us with the usual friendly smiles, which I find it difficult not to respond to.

'Mm, this smells good,' Mo says, picking up his spoon. 'So how did you get on at the market?'

I tell him, warts and all.

He listens in silence, his jaws slowly masticating. He is more intent on savouring the taste of his chicken curry than hearing about the fate of some unfortunate pig. 'At least the pigs were already dead,' I go on. 'Everything else that could not be labelled mineral or vegetable was still alive. It was awful.' He throws me a glance after I finish the bit about the fish but then keeps on eating.

I am determined to get him to at least put his fork down. The part about the chicken only has him pause for a minute to take a drink of water. Convinced he is not listening, I go on to the frogs. The effect is to make him squirm around the chicken he is busy chewing. I have chosen a Thai soup, knowing that it was made with prawns, which are sufficiently divorced from my emotions for me to be able to eat them. However, I seem only to have succeeded in putting myself off even these. I push the soup away and take a sip of water.

'I thought you liked the food here?' he says, eyeing my abandoned soup.

'I do, it just takes a bit of getting used to. It's quite a different taste.' Pride will not allow me to admit to being squeamish now.

'Yes, but you enjoyed your dinner last night?'

'Yes, it was really good.'

'The chicken, the pork?'

'Yes.' I feel a sense of wariness creeping over me.

'And you haven't felt ill?'

'No.' I am very wary now.

'So where do you think the hotels buy their food?'

Of course, I see what he is getting at: we are a long way from Bangkok; there are no supermarkets selling meat and poultry, so all the food we have eaten so far has come from the market, and in my blissful ignorance I have had no qualms about eating it.

'OK, point taken,' I concede reluctantly, knowing when I am beat. At least I have a week's grace before I must tackle the food problem on my own.

'You're just going to have to get used to it, dear.' He throws me a half-understanding smile as he glances at his watch. 'I've got to get back to the office. You should go and lie down for a bit. Take it easy until you get used to the heat.' He bends over to kiss my brow where it hurts.

I sigh heavily. 'Yes, OK.' I force a bright smile. My eyes follow him as he walks towards the door. It is all right for him; he is not going to have to go to the bloody market.

CHAPTER THREE

That evening we decide to go for a drink after dinner. I'm keen to meet people and Mo is anxious to introduce me to everyone.

'Most of the *farangs* go to a pub in town owned by an expat called Guy and his Thai wife, Mimi,' he tells me. 'It's the only place in town where the music doesn't tax the eardrums.'

I feel bubbles of excitement playing in my stomach as we park under the trees in the dusty car park in front of the pub and make our way towards the single-storey building, its lights shining through the pitch-black night.

'It's usually busier than this.' Mo sounds disappointed as we realise there are only two *farangs* there: a middle-aged couple, perched on bar stools on one side of the horseshoe-shaped bar.

I'm surprised to see that it's just like any pub back home really. Tall stools are dotted around the bar, red-and-white-checked-clothed tables flank either side, and the walls are covered in old, framed photographs. Shelves of paperback books line one section of a wall; next to that is a panel holding foreign banknotes and above this is a photograph of the King and Queen of Thailand next to a small altar attached to the wall. On the opposite wall is a large map of the world and next to it a dartboard where a Thai couple are amusing themselves playing darts. Between the bar and the door is a U-shaped island bar with stools providing extra seating.

Mo introduces me to Tom and Eva, who sit with their elbows set dejectedly on the bar adjacent to where we decide to sit at the top end so we can all see each other. 'Tom works for the oil company.' Tom's smile seems genuine enough if somewhat strained, his wife Eva gives a flick of her wrist and, with a ghost of a smile, says hello. Not the best ingredients for an enjoyable night out. I wonder what's wrong?

'Good evening, Khun Mo.' A pretty Thai girl whom Mo introduces as Mui beams a smile at both of us as we lever our respective bottoms onto stools. 'No have, sorree. Maybe come tomorrow,' Mui apologises when I ask for a white wine. I swallow my disappointment and ask for a beer instead. Mo has already warned me that wine is difficult to get here and now, in the current welcoming climate, I wonder how on earth I am going to do without it.

'Khun Guy, Khun Mimi?' Mo asks as Mui sets out the glasses.

'Go Bangkok, come back tomorrow,' Mui tells him.

Mo and Tom begin to talk, and since it's difficult to have a conversation with Eva, who is sitting on the other side of Tom and doesn't seem in the mood to be chatty, my eyes are drawn to the bookshelves, which would normally act like a magnet, but I curtail my impulses so as not to appear rude. Another part of the wall I notice is devoted to business cards and various photographs are dotted around.

An island set behind the bar houses a display of drinks on offer, and for a while I try to comfort myself perusing the various labels, musing over which one might act as substitute for my beloved wine.

At the same time, as usual, I keep half an ear on the men's conversation, occasionally joining in. After a while there is one of those empty silences when people have run out of things to say. Eva, who has been studiously toying with her drink all evening, suddenly lets out a huge sigh.

'Well,' she says, raising her eyebrows and blinking slowly, 'I suppose one ought to ask the question.' She pauses for effect. 'How do you like living here?'

Stunned for a moment by this sudden attention, I am lost for words, then the jet-lag irritation takes over. 'Actually, I've only just arrived, but so far it seems to be OK.' By this time, I feel no urge to follow this up with my usual smile.

My reply is met with a raised eyebrow. Tom, I notice, stares fixedly into his glass.

'If I ever show a hint of getting to be like that, I want you to promise me you'll get me out of here,' I tell Mo as we make our way later towards the car.

'Sorry. It isn't usually like that. It was a bad night; anyway, they are oil people and they have their own problems. She isn't the only woman here.'

Yes, but what are the others going to be like? I wonder. *Surely it can't be that bad.*

'There aren't many expats,' Mo says as we drive back to the hotel. 'Most of them work for the oil company.' I lunge sideways as he swerves to avoid a dog lying curled up on the road. 'It's just sleeping – they like the heat from the road,' he explains as I crane my head to look.

'There are two oil couples living in the hotel. One couple seem friendly, Cookie and her husband Joe. Joe works offshore so Cookie is on her own most of the time. She goes down to the pub quite a bit, just for the company. We've had a good laugh some nights. They have visitors at the moment, though. Wouldn't do any harm to introduce yourself when you get the chance. You'll have to make the effort. People aren't going to come to you,' he says ominously.

'What about the other couple?'

'They are young and newly married, I believe. The other oil people live on a compound outside town, so you won't necessarily see much of them. They aren't exactly the friendliest bunch of people I've met.'

'So I've noticed.'

Down in the lobby the next morning on my way to buy the *Bangkok Post* – which, I am told, is in English – I bump into Khun Pornsak, the hotel manager.

'*Sawadee krap*, madame.' Khun Pornsak flashes his come-to-bed eyes as he approaches me.

'*Sawadee kha.*' I smile and answer with the female version of 'hello' in Thai, ending with a tone of surprise, as the waitresses have taught me. He murmurs something in Thai, which I don't understand. I stare back at him blankly. His face creases into a seductive smile. 'You learn to speak Thai?'

'Yes, well, I want to learn, but so far I can only say a few words.' He gives me an understanding nod. 'I will teach you a new phrase every day. Then you will soon speak Thai,' he assures me before he is mercifully called away; my brain isn't ready for impromptu phrases just now.

I buy the paper and go back upstairs, by which time the maids have arrived. I hand them Mo's navy-blue Jaeger trousers bought in a sale, plus the form that I have filled in for them to be dry-cleaned, and then decide on impulse to kill two birds with one stone. I remember Mo talking about the newly married couple that haven't been here for very long, so I decide I'll ask the wife if she wants to go with me to the market.

I try to ignore the nervous flutter in my stomach that always arrives at the thought of meeting anyone new and, taking a deep breath that lifts my boobs up to the position I wish they occupied permanently, I ring the doorbell.

'Hi. I'm Mo's wife,' I say as cheerily as I can muster to the tall, pale-skinned woman who opens the door. 'I'm just off down to the market and I wondered if you'd like to go?'

Her dark hair is pulled back from an attractive face with a rather aloof, vacant expression. 'Actually, I have everything I need,' she answers in a slightly accented voice. 'But would you like to come in and have a coffee? I'm Monique,' she says politely.

'Oh, OK, thanks.' I leap at the chance and follow as Monique leads the way into the small apartment.

It takes only a shocked few seconds to register that the neatly coiffed blonde-haired woman sitting at the dining table carefully set for morning coffee is Eva. The tablecloth, I can't help noticing, is pristine white. 'Hello,' I say, and force a smile, trying to float my sinking heart.

Oh God, I think, and wish I hadn't bothered.

I note that Eva's smile is more enthusiastic; maybe it will be OK after all. I cling to the hope.

Monique invites me to sit down opposite Eva, then disappears into the kitchen. After a few minutes, she reappears with a coffee pot.

My first thought is that everything matches: the coffee pot, the cups, saucers and plates, and there in the middle of the table is a cake, a perfectly baked cake. I can tell, because it isn't smothered in icing the way mine always must be to hide the potholes, as Mo calls them.

It suddenly occurs to me that Mo and I have only just managed to complete our dinner set that had started out as a breakfast set years ago and I have left it all behind in the house for other people to use. Seized with a sudden bout of anger with myself, I clutch the seat of my chair then press my lips tightly together; this is not something to air in the present company.

Like examiners presiding over a domestic science practical, Eva and I watch in silence as Monique pours the coffee into the cup with the precision of a factory robot, her face displaying a professional detachment, one eyebrow arched tensely and the fingers of one hand carefully balanced on the lid. Not a drop spills. I am filled with admiration. She hands me the cup and saucer.

'How are you settling in?' Eva asks quietly.

'Oh. OK,' I say, declining the offer of a piece of cake from Monique. 'Still trying to get organised and find my way around.'

'Yes, we know what that's like, don't we?' Eva turns her attention to Monique, who nods in agreement. The atmosphere is laced with an awkwardness I can't define, then I realise, after a while, that they are having a conversation almost designed to exclude me. *Oh God,* I wail silently, suddenly longing for coffee mugs and the cheerful banter of my friends and colleagues back home.

'How long have you been here?' I stare pointedly at Monique, wondering if I'm being overly sensitive.

'Only a few months.' She takes a sip of her coffee. 'We arranged the wedding when we heard that Jacques was to be posted out here. There was no time for a honeymoon.'

'At least you came straight to the apartment; you didn't have to stay in that dreadful hotel we were all put into when we arrived,' Eva suddenly cuts in, taking me completely by surprise. 'It was crawling with cockroaches.' She shudders, her face creased with distaste. 'We all ended up with the runs. I've never been so ill in all my life. Of course, we know who is responsible for that,' she goes on.

I now wonder who the nameless person was but decide not to ask. 'Will you be moving to the housing compound?' I blurt out to change the subject, mentally trying to obliterate the thought of those cockroaches.

Monique stiffens, her large, sombre eyes becoming aloof. 'Not at the moment.'

'You ought to; it's a disgrace that you're stuck here away from everyone else.' An awkward silence follows as everyone considers this. I decide that pursuing the current topic will only lead to grief and search my brain frantically for something else to say.

Then, just as if a director had shouted action, Eva suddenly grips her wrist and peers down at her watch. Her eyes flick across to Monique. 'Forty-five minutes, was it? Right,' she says decisively.

I watch in amazement as Eva gets up, closely followed by Monique, and then, without uttering a word, the two women disappear into the kitchen. It strikes me that I had the same feeling when I went to see one of Harold Pinter's plays – a complete lack of understanding as to what was going on.

I consider for a moment whether I ought to leave. *No, dammit, I won't*, I tell myself, and begin to look around the room, contemplating the hotel's blue-and-white-striped, rattan furniture and comforting myself with the conclusion that it is marginally worse than the company's contribution Mo and I are stuck with. They do have a blue carpet, newer than our brown one, and their own bits and pieces make it seem quite homely compared to our comparatively empty mansion.

As my eyes roam around they fall on a large effigy of a Buddhist monk, sitting on the floor in the corner, portraying a state of blissful meditation. *Oh God, I wish that were me*, I think longingly.

The rest of the room reveals nothing of spectacular interest and the monk isn't about to strike up conversation, so, after several minutes and feeling irritated now, I get up and march across to the kitchen door.

Eva and Monique are standing by the cooker in the tiny kitchen, leaning over a pot of something simmering on the cooker between them. 'You should taste it now and see if it needs salt,' Eva's voice instructs.

'What's cooking?' I breeze in, determined now not to be ignored.

Eva's eyes are intent on Monique as she sips some liquid from the wooden spoon. 'OK?'

'Mm.' Monique licks her lips clinically. 'It's OK.' I wait stubbornly.

'It's a goulash.' Monique addresses me at last. 'I must learn how to cook, so Eva comes every day to teach me.' This all fits in with the chapter in the book my friend lent me.

'You can switch it off now,' Eva announces, and she walks past me. I follow in the wake of the two women as they traipse back into the lounge and resume their seating positions.

Eva says suddenly, 'Don't forget to see the company doctor when he comes up to give his talk.' Her face displays a look of concern. 'Tell him what's wrong,' she adds cryptically.

'What's the talk about?' I pipe up, genuinely interested and knowing I am excluded from whatever is wrong with Monique.

'Oh,' Eva pauses, 'it's, ah… it's for the wives. It's about how to cope with living in this kind of environment.'

'I'd be interested in that,' I venture. 'Would it be possible for me to go along?'

'I don't see why not,' Eva says, surprising me. 'I'll ask Tom.'

At this point the doorbell goes and another oil wife arrives on the scene. Her name is Frances. She sits down and briefly acknowledges my presence. 'Oh, you're Kitty's replacement,' she says. I don't much like being compared to a spare part, but I do my best to ignore the terminology. 'Yes, she'd had enough – she was more than ready to go, wasn't she?' Frances says cryptically to the others.

She then starts talking about her leave and I sit, ever the spectator, listening politely and wondering why the hell Kitty was so anxious to go.

It seems that another topic of conversation that from now on will rear its head continually is the fact that the company have omitted to build a squash court, which apparently is essential to everyone's health and happiness. This becomes such an obsession with these people I am sorely tempted to write to their MD myself, just to shut everybody up. After a while Eva excuses herself; she has some housework to do, she tells us. Frances says she has promised Grace, the Canadian lady who also lives in the hotel, that she will go up and have a coffee with her. Grace is anxious for some company, so Frances thinks Monique should go as well. At that point I am not included.

I sit on for some stubborn reason I can't quite fathom. Finally, Frances says they must go, and would I like to join them, which I realise is what I've been waiting for.

Grace is a lovely woman. Older than the rest of us, but so welcoming I wish I'd skipped the middle women and gone there first. She also has her great-niece Beth staying with her. We spend a very pleasant half hour and then, hungry for lunch, we leave. I decide to go to have a bowl of noodles in the coffee shop. 'Didn't realise Grace had her niece staying with her,' Frances suddenly says on the way down in the lift. 'I won't have to worry about her now.'

I wonder what this is oil speak for but decline to ask; my stomach is rumbling from all that coffee.

That evening Mo arrives back with the computer manual. 'I just thought you might want to have a read of it first to familiarise yourself,' he says hopefully.

'Of course,' I say, pleased to have something else to think about.

'I fancy going to the pub tonight,' he says, and I am relieved that I won't have to spend the entire evening reading a computer manual because the TV programmes are all in Thai.

'This is more like it,' Mo murmurs as he guides me across the parking area in front of the pub. It's very dark now and the warm, still air is heavy with the piercing trill of cicadas.

'Sounds like a referees' night out,' I quip as we pick our way across the dusty ground. The lights from the pub are shining invitingly through the clear windows and I note with a flutter of anticipation that quite a few people are gathered round the bar.

'Looks like the regulars are back,' Mo says eagerly. I take a deep, boob-lifting breath.

As soon as we walk in, I can tell that the atmosphere matches my own mood; even the lights seem brighter.

'I warn you,' Mo says as we approach the effusive greetings, 'most of them come straight from work so they're well-oiled by this time, no pun intended.'

An attractive Thai lady comes towards us. 'Good evening, Khun Mo. I am very pleased to meet you,' she says as she is introduced to me. 'Please come and have a dring.' She flashes another smile at Mo. This is Mimi, who owns the pub with her husband Guy.

As we approach the crowded bar, a tall, slim, white-haired man sitting at the corner of the bar extends his hand. 'Hello, I'm Guy,' he says as Mo introduces me. 'It's good to meet you. Welcome to our pub.'

'Good to meet you too,' I say, shaking his hand. As I am led around, various names are churned out. I shake each hand in turn, trying hard to concentrate above the noise. Mo has talked about these people so often they feel quite familiar. The ones who come in straight from work are known as the sundowners and it isn't difficult to spot who they are. The glassy eyes and slightly slurred speech are a dead giveaway.

'Hello, Mo. How's things?' A pleasant-looking man who appears to be in his thirties suddenly notices us and breaks off his conversation. 'Hello, Mo's wife, pleased to meet you,' he says, shaking my hand heartily. This is Theo, one of the contractors (those who are not the oil company people but work for them). Sitting beside him is Max, who, I remember teaches English. 'Nice to see a new face.' He beams as we are introduced. 'Welcome to the madhouse. You don't have to be mad to drink here, but it helps.'

I am invited to sit on an empty stool.

'Khun Mo, wha would you lie to dring?' Mui asks.

'A Klosters, and…?' He looks at me.

'You have white wine?' I ask, not daring to hope.

'*Wai see kao?* Have,' Mui declares triumphantly with a huge smile.

A phrase not to be forgotten, I repeat it over and over like a silent mantra and watch in anticipation as she opens the cooler. Noting the two-litre bottle, my heart sinks a little. Ever since we rented a row of vines in France a couple of years ago, we have hitherto jokingly labelled any white wine in a jumbo-sized bottle as elephants' piss.

Given the alternatives, I am more than happy to slum it. The local whisky is called Mekhong. It's hellfire in a bottle and packs a dangerous punch. Rumour has it that it stalks around in your body and then strikes when you least expect it. But it's cheap, which is probably the only reason for its popularity. Theo mixes it with Coke, and I wonder if this is either to drown the taste or because it gives it an added kick, or perhaps both. He has a share in the establishment with Guy and Mimi and does his bit by propping up the bar each evening, encouraged by Mimi, to make sure that his money goes towards a worthy cause.

The place is fairly packed now, and the hum of voices is turning into more of a din as it rises in proportion to the amount of alcohol being consumed. Smoke is curling round like early morning fog. I am introduced to Ziggy from East Germany and his wife Anna. A little later I find myself listening enthralled as Ziggy describes his escape to the West. It seems that he escaped in a bus. I am finding it increasingly difficult to follow his story and am grateful when a hand touches my shoulder and a tall, slim lady who introduces herself as Cookie claims my attention.

'It's good to meet you,' she says in a slightly accented voice. 'Like you I stay in the hotel, but I have been away for a while. How are you? Has anyone shown you around?' She frowns with the effort of trying to hear herself speak.

'Well, not really,' I begin hesitantly.

Cookie puts a comforting hand on my shoulder. 'Oh, but I know what it is like to be alone here.' She nods gravely. 'My husband is away most of the time and I am stuck in this place,' she says, sweeping her eyes around. 'Before it was terrible, but now I have the car so I can drive. I have visitors now, but when they have gone, I will show you around. I'll introduce you to the ladies,' she promises ominously. 'I have to go now; I can't bear to hear Ziggy escaping yet again and this noise is giving me a headache. But I will see you later, OK?' She flashes me an encouraging smile and I, feeling slightly bemused but decidedly cheered, manage to stammer, 'OK.'

Ziggy, meanwhile, has elevated his position to that of ex-fighter pilot, then mentions the KGB. Max is thumping the bar, declaring himself to be the only true expat because he lives and works here on a local salary. 'Rubbish,' Theo retorts, grinning at him, unaware that his drooping fag ash is about to fall into his Mekhong Coke.

Anyone standing near the dartboard is now in danger of being hit by a dart bouncing off the board as the professionals stop to begin some serious drinking and the more inebriated amateurs take over.

'Khun Mo, you wan anudder dring?' Mui is primed to hover near any glass that is almost empty and make sure it is filled again as soon as possible. Mo is looking happy but still, I hope, just sober enough to drive home, and if I have another one, I'll be peeing reconstituted elephants' piss all night. We agree it's time to drag ourselves away.

My first Saturday in Pits is spent in the office with my bum on a chair sitting in front of the computer all day trying to figure out the instructions left by Mo's predecessor. We have waited until the Saturday as Mo's office is in the oil company building and he isn't sure how they will react to a wife being around. However, the monthly printout is due soon and we must do something about it.

I am suspicious of the computer, which has come from Singapore and is not a make I recognise, so we get off to a bad start.

It soon becomes clear that some vital stages in the instructions have been omitted and we are well and truly stuck. I have never used this software before; Mo's secretary Nok and Ying, the girl who does the filing, are hovering around nervously. I have already had two coffees and the atmosphere is getting tense.

When I decline a third cup, Nok asks sweetly, 'Would madame lie cha jeen?' I perk up, smile and say thanks, I'd love one. Then I must hide my disappointment when I discover this is not the offer of a gin as I had thought but Chinese tea.

The atmosphere is becoming decidedly more tense as the morning wears on. Ying, whose bladder would seem to be even worse than mine, keeps running off to the loo, and Nok has made us so many cups of Chinese tea I feel bloated. We stop for lunch and then continue late into the afternoon.

On the Monday morning, it occurs to me that Khun Mo's Jaeger trousers have not yet come back, so I make enquiries. Nim, who seems to be the more senior maid, frowns and says she will go look. Later that afternoon she finally appears with Mo's trousers, which are looking decidedly crumpled. I try to contain my horror and demand that they are taken back and pressed. An hour later I discover that it doesn't do to try to hurry anything and regret my impatience, as the trousers that are handed over now bear scant resemblance to the ones I gave them a few days ago. Not only are they badly pressed but they also have shiny streaks over all the seams, which I know means that these lovely trousers, that Mo was so pleased to have found in the sale, are well and truly ruined.

'What have you done to them?' I throw up my hands in despair but quickly realise that Nim hasn't a clue why I am so upset. When I show them to Mo later, he simply shrugs his shoulders philosophically and says, 'Ah well.' I later discover that the hotels don't do dry-cleaning, so the trousers had been washed. This is when I find out that there is only one dry-cleaning place in town. The trials and tribulations of the newly arrived.

Zeb, the big boss from Singapore, comes to pay a visit. He seems pleasant and tells me that if I want to move out of the hotel and stay in a house, he won't have any objection.

The next Friday is a holiday so we end up in the office all day and go back on the Saturday, by which time we seem to have solved the problem. The tension and tiredness melt away as we stand together, like proud parents, watching the machine churn out the longed-for monthly printout.

All goes well until page fifteen, when, for some unknown reason, the printer starts playing silly buggers and the print comes out in huge letters. It is impossible to start again at page sixteen, so we must go back to the beginning. I could weep. 'Stupid bloody machine.'

'Don't blame the machine; we've obviously done something wrong.'

Ying and Nok are hovering nervously again, and we've drunk so many cups of cha jeen we'll be peeing green for a fortnight.

'I've never had this much trouble with computers at work,' I try to reason. 'There must be something wrong with it.'

'You've done nothing but complain about it since you arrived. If you don't want to help, just say so!'

'I do,' I protest, inwardly furious. I am about to tell him that he should be bloody grateful I'm doing this at all when I catch sight of Ying hovering in the doorway looking as though she either has or is about to wet her knickers. I force myself to smile. Why on earth is this girl so nervous?

I search my brain, then it hits me. Thai people don't do this kind of thing. By engaging in a fishwives' exchange Mo and I are 'losing face'. I heave a sigh and start trying to calm us both down. Luckily, we get the thing going again and the monthly printout emerges, this time without any hitches.

That night, our better natures restored, we decide to celebrate by going for a drink to one of the bars on the river. We literally walk the plank over mud and water to get to it. To my dismay they don't sell wine and I'm not a beer fan, so I opt for the Mekhong. It isn't possible to buy it by the glass for some reason, so I must buy a half bottle. This is OK because it seems to be the custom to drink what you want and then leave the bottle for the next time. Quite how they keep track I don't know. It doesn't taste anywhere near as strong as whisky, and as it turns out, by the time we decide to leave, not much of it is left.

I am fine until I stand up and then realise my brain is having trouble connecting with my legs. I walk with the mustered dignity of the inebriated and only with Mo's helping hand do I manage to negotiate the narrow plank back to the riverbank and climb the steps up the steep slope to the road.

'What you need is some food,' Mo declares, and guides me to the nearest riverboat restaurant. We order some curry and rice, which turns out to be so hot we can't eat it all and finally must give up and go home. The next morning, I wake up with a head that feels like it has been hit with a sledgehammer and swear never to drink again.

Sod it, I curse silently amidst the throng of stalls and people around me as the plank of wood I am negotiating suddenly sinks beneath my weight, allowing the warm, muddy liquid to seep over my toes. Stupid to have worn these sandals when no self-respecting Thai person would have ventured forth in anything other than a pair of rubber flip-flops, which seem to be de rigueur for daywear in these parts.

I am beginning to deeply regret my earlier decision to come out specially to use my Thai to buy something on my own. To make matters worse, the cooling effect of the earlier rainstorm is beginning to wear off as the sun mops up the moisture with the fierce determination of an angry cleaning lady.

Aroon has been taking me down to another market, which is on the next street parallel to the first market we went to. He introduced me to his friend, who sells a large variety of vegetables. I fell on a stack of potatoes like long-lost friends and baked and stuffed them with my limited repertoire of ideas until they ran out and Mo finally asked if we could have something else for dinner.

Having been to the market already this morning with Aroon, I don't need any more vegetables. Tonight, we are going to have soup for a change. I am also feeling insanely pleased with myself because Aroon took me to a small bakery in a shophouse near the market and I was amazed to see a pile of wholemeal rolls.

This is a major triumph, because the Thai people love everything sweet and so the bread is all white and sweet to cater for their taste. I have an abhorrence of all foods of the white variety and have already had to accept that all the rice that's eaten here is white.

'Specia odda,' the baker, a young, tall, handsome man of the M&B variety tells me but kindly allows me to have four. 'I would like same order for me,' I tell him, thinking with a spur of excitement that I can put them in the fridge-freezer. The soup will last two days. Things are looking up. So, I order some '*see namtan my sai namtam*' which translates as crusty rolls, hamburger bun shape, colour brown, i.e., wholemeal, no sugar. Thai is a tonal language, so the same word is used for sugar and the colour brown, only different tones. This phrase becomes another one of my mantras.

Unfortunately, it is the rainy season, and an earlier surge of rain, of Niagara proportions, has left the ground decidedly muddy. I pick my way carefully between the crowded rows of stalls selling mainly fruit and vegetables, but no matter how hard I try to avoid it, my feet are getting muddier by the minute. I look down at the patches of grey sludge and despair of ever getting my white, sling-back sandals clean again.

Aroon has always taken me a different way where there are paving stones, but my sense of direction has let me down as usual. *Damn*, I curse silently, and then feel a sudden rush of irritation as a passing bike splatters another dollop of mud onto my ankle. *Well, too bad*, I tell myself impatiently. *You might as well make it worthwhile and at least buy something.* The next stall I come to sells bananas. The sheer number of bananas lying or hanging in huge bunches, whose colours range from a vivid green through to a vibrant sunny yellow, is mind-boggling. They completely fill the stall, lining all three walls and covering most of the earthen floor. I search my brain frantically for the Thai word for bananas.

One of the women in charge of the stall beckons to me. I smile and then force the smile in place as the woman's mouth gapes back at me in the garish, crimson, betel-clogged grin sported by a few of the older Thai women who are addicted to chewing betel nut. The very sight of this wet, bloody, gaping hole makes me want to gag.

My instinct is to move on quickly, but the two other women have warmed to the task now and are beckoning me and smiling encouragement. I smile back and stubbornly continue to walk past, picking my way along strategically placed pieces of wood. Silently I curse a motorcyclist who comes from behind and brushes past me, sending up a fresh volume of mud. Then I stop and think for a minute. This should be easy; at least there won't be any mistaking what I want. I pat my handbag, assured by the knowledge that my phrasebook is inside. However, I decide it is important that they don't take me for a tourist; after all, I do have to shop here for the next three years, and I don't want everybody thinking I'm a soft touch.

So, like a spy on location, I try to mingle nonchalantly with the passing crowd and get in the way of a man pedalling behind a cyclist's equivalent of a forklift truck overloaded with a haystack of vegetables of the green variety and designed with volume in mind rather than movement. He seems oblivious to anything other than what is happening up front of his machine. As this machine on wheels brushes past it's like going through the equivalent of a vegetarian car wash only coming out filthy instead of clean.

None of the passing Thai people seem to mind, but then they are more sensibly dressed in jeans or dark trousers and coloured tops, not my light-coloured shorts. Aware now that I must look like the rugby player who has ended up at the bottom of the scrum, I do my best to wipe off the worst of the mud then give up, find a spot between two stalls, where I feel less conspicuous, open my handbag, locate the small phrasebook and surreptitiously begin to flick through the pages until I find the word for bananas.

Uncomfortably aware of the sun mercilessly targeting my exposed parts of flesh, not to mention the sweat trickling its way downwards between my breasts, I study the text quickly and then shove the book down into my bag. I practise the word a few times in my head and then casually wander back through the mingling crowd, trying to avoid any further spattering and fighting the feeling of being as conspicuous as a giraffe in a field of midgets.

As I get closer to the stall the women spy me immediately and are frantic now, waving their arms excitedly. 'OK. OK.' I laugh. This is it. I take a deep breath. 'I would like six bananas,' I say solemnly in Thai, and hold up six fingers so there can be no mistake.

Whatever I expected, it wasn't this reaction, as all three women look collectively stunned for a moment and then fall about laughing.

I smile doubtfully; surely, they understand. I try saying it again, displaying six fingers as before, but this only brings a fresh bout of laughter.

Trying my best to ignore the stares of passers-by, my lips remain spliced in a patient smile. 'One more time,' I mutter to myself, beads of sweat dripping into my eyes, wishing for once that the heat from the sun would melt me away. This time I pronounce the word for bananas twice and hold up six fingers.

This throws the women into hysterics, two of them clutching each other for support and one squatting alarmingly on the ground, her face screwed up in that concentrated way that makes me fear for the state of her knickers.

Totally baffled now, I can only stare at them in amazement. The squatting woman finally manages to contain herself, gets up and, advancing with a monkey-like gait that suggests my worst fears have been confirmed, picks out an enormous bunch of small bananas, puts them in a bag, touches me with a mothering gesture on the arm and says, '*Hah baht*,' which I know for sure means five baht.

This can't be right, I think, as I hand the money over, anxious to get away as soon as possible, *and I don't want all these bloody bananas*. I open my mouth to protest, but the woman, overtaken by a fresh bout of giggling, waves me away.

'What on earth possessed you to buy all these bananas?' Mo says, as I have been predicting he would, when he walks in from work. The offending bunch is lying on the kitchen top and seems to be ripening as we speak.

'I didn't mean to; I only asked for six bananas,' I tell him, and, still smarting from my embarrassment, describe what happened. 'This lot only cost five baht, so they must have thought it was funny me wanting only six when they are so cheap, I suppose.' I shrug. 'I mean, it's only the equivalent of about eight pence in our money. Anyway,' I let out a sigh of irritation, 'I'll know the next time.'

'What's for dinner?' I can see Mo eyeing the pot with a ray of hope.

'Vegetable soup,' I tell him curtly.

'Oh.' He lets out a sigh. 'I'm going to have a shower,' he says, sounding really disappointed.

'I've got wholemeal rolls,' I cry out to him encouragingly. Mo really prefers white rolls but I'm working on it.

The next morning Aroon parks the car as close as he possibly can to the baker's shop in the street that serves as an outside market from 5am until 8am each day, by which time all traces of market debris are swept and hosed away. It is still only half past seven, so, closely followed by Aroon, I have to run the gauntlet of the market vendors sitting on the pavement smiling good-humouredly and groping my legs to get my attention.

For the sake of peace, I stop to buy some fruit under the eagle eye of Aroon, who hovers like a demented mother bird lest I be overcharged. I tiptoe my way through the fast-rotting remains of that morning's produce, trip over a piece of metal sticking up through the concrete and narrowly miss falling over two boys squatting on the pavement playing a board game with old bottle tops. When I finally get to the baker's shop, I think the poor baker has suffered drastic weight loss overnight until I realise it is a different man.

The new baker grins, creasing his cheeks into concertina-like folds, I note, on either side of his emaciated face. I open my mouth to ask about the rolls I have ordered when a curtain in the corner is drawn aside, revealing the baker I know, naked apart from a towel around his waist.

He looks startled and then embarrassed. My mind immediately shifts into M&B writer's mode, and I suddenly realise my eyes are firmly locked on to his dark, toffee-coloured nipples.

'My bruzzer,' he says, pointing to the emaciated-looking man as if trying to divert my attention.

'Ah.' I nod and smile to the man. 'The rolls?' I raise my eyebrows hopefully.

Maybe four o'clock.' He smiles uncomfortably.

'OK.' I grin, backing out whilst trying hard to keep my eyes fixed on his face.

'We go office now, Aroon,' I say briskly. Aroon, who has been having a quick fag, stubs it out with his foot and rushes round to open the car door for me. He does this with the careful concentration and the delicate precision of someone opening a safe. He never ever yanks the door open and seems to live in fear of me getting to it first. Once I am inside, he carefully presses the door closed.

When we reach the office building, Aroon gets out and quickly rushes round to open the door with the same precision he used to close it. Even if I manage to open the door before he does, he makes sure I don't get to close it, or, as Mo would put it, slam it shut.

I sign in and collect my visitor's badge under the fatherly supervision of Aroon, who, having sussed out my vagueness from early on in our relationship, has assumed the role of minder as well as driver.

Nok is sitting frowning at the computer screen. 'Why?' she asks the screen.

'You have a problem?'

'Oh, madame.' She smiles. 'Would madame lie some coffee?'

'No, thank you.' I have a look at what she is doing. She has spellcheck on the go but doesn't know which word to choose.

The day before I spent some time showing her how to type a letter on the computer from scratch, but so far, she has only known how to call up a letter and change a few words where necessary. This letter looks new; I am impressed. 'You did this letter yourself?'

'Yessir.' She beams a smile. For some reason I can't fathom why both girls always say this when either of us asks them a question.

'Well done. Why not use the dictionary?' I suggest, which she duly does. However, it is obvious from the deepening frown lines that she doesn't understand, so I explain and suggest which word to use.

'Thank you, madame.' She giggles nervously and I leave her to carry on whilst I go over to Mo's desk to read the paper and wait for him to return. 'Madame?'

'Yes?'

'I don know. Why?' Nok says, frowning at the screen again a few minutes later.

I go across. It's spellcheck again, querying a word. My heart sinks. It's the same word that was in the paragraph before. She has absolutely no understanding of what she is doing. I then discover that the letter isn't a new one at all; it's simply one that she has called up as usual. The couple of hours I spent with her yesterday were totally wasted. She must have said she understood merely to please me. Thus, I learn a valuable lesson – to admit to not knowing something means loss of face. Never believe anything you are told.

'You eat crap?' the young baker asks matily when I walk into the small bakery to collect my rolls at the agreed time. My mental processing does an emergency stop, leaving me wide-eyed and open-mouthed. *He's getting his own back*, is my thought. I manage an indulgent smile; perhaps he's had a bad holiday in the UK.

'You know crap?' he persists amiably, wiping his floury hands on his yellow-white apron with the confidence of one who is fully dressed.

'Um.' Oh dear. I begin mentally changing gear, my eyes darting around the small, flour-dusted shop, searching for something to link the word with amongst the array of cakes and bread displayed under the glass counter. 'Thai word,' I affirm, raising my eyes hopefully.

'No. Eengliss. Crap.' I am watching his lips carefully, taking into account that the Thais barely pronounce the last letter of a word, but there is no mistaking what he had said.

'You no eat?'

I flinch at the suggestion, my eyes wide with alarm. A Thai woman and her young daughter wander in and begin to take an interest in the bread and cakes.

'Same, selfiss,' he persists, ignoring his new customers. He looks round impatiently and then picks up a piece of paper and a pen and begins to write the word.

I hold my breath, eyes glued to the letters. *Oh God*, I wail silently as the crudely written letter P confirms my worst fears.

'You know selfiss?' he tries again with an incredulous frown. 'Crap, selfiss.' *Selfish?* My mind is struggling to get the connection.

'Yeh, eat?' he persists.

The Thai lady and her daughter mercifully have now decided on their choice and insist on attention. I begin to feel desperate, playing the words over and over silently in my mind. Then it twigs. 'Oh! Shellfish. You mean crab!' I almost faint with relief.

'Yeh, crap.' He grins, stuffing a loaf of bread into the woman's bag.

CHAPTER FOUR

I decide to visit Grace and take her some rolls. The apartment she and Harry have is furnished with the hotel standard blue- and-white-striped rattan suite. Both this apartment and Monique's have a blue carpet, so everything matches. Grace is obviously a collector, judging by the plethora of ornaments dotted around the room.

'How are you settling in?' Grace appears, carrying a tray, which she sets down carefully on the coffee table.

'Oh, slowly but surely,' I say, thinking that the soup will last one more day and then I really will have to buy Mo something a bit more substantial.

'Don't you just hate going to the market?' Grace asks as she hands me a cup of coffee.

'Well, it does take a bit of getting used to,' I admit.

'I don't think I'll ever get used to it. I only go when I have to. I have some Thai friends who are very kind and go for me sometimes.'

I make a mental note to cultivate some Thai friends. 'It's so dirty.' She shakes her head. 'Sometimes I just don't understand how anything works in this country. Incidentally, they don't kill the pigs on religious days. If you don't see the pigs' heads swinging around that means the meat isn't fresh, so don't buy it.'

God, that would be a relief, I think. 'I haven't actually plucked up the courage to buy anything like that yet,' I admit sheepishly.

'Well, I must confess that we cheat and buy our meat in Bangkok. The meat here is tough, so we have chicken, but I do hate if I have to buy it myself. I appreciate the rolls, though, they're so much better for you.' I have an ally at last.

We sip our coffee in companionable silence, only broken by the trundling of the AC unit. I notice a column of ants making its way purposefully up the wall at the side of the kitchen door. 'They're moving house,' Grace explains. 'I've been watching them all morning.'

I tear my eyes away. 'Is Harry out of town much?'

Grace presses her lips together. 'Monday to Friday quite a lot of the time,' she says finally. 'I could stay down where he is working but there's even less for me to do there. At least I know people here and the hotel staff are wonderful. You don't play bridge, do you?' Her eyes gleam with hope.

'No, sorry.' I smile wanly, watching the gleam fade under a cloud of disappointment. 'My brain can't concentrate on that kind of thing,' I add, wishing this revelation didn't make me feel such a heel.

'I used to play bridge with the oil ladies the last time we were here, but they don't seem to play now for some reason. At least I've never been invited. Perhaps they have enough women who play now. I think some of them have been replaced. Maybe the new women don't play. Or maybe they don't need me to make up the numbers.'

'Oh.' I lift my coffee cup to take another sip, pondering over this.

'Yes, it helped to pass the time, I used to enjoy it.' Grace looks wistful. 'Frances used to invite me round to her house a lot. I got to know her maid very well, but I haven't seen nor heard from her since you were all here for coffee.' She shrugs her shoulders.

'Some of them don't seem particularly happy,' I venture. 'I have to admit I find them a bit strange; there's something not right. I just can't put my finger on it, but I'm not going to lose any sleep over it.'

'Me neither.' Grace gets up. 'I'm going to pour another cup of coffee. Would you like some?'

'No, thanks.' I shake my head as she disappears off into the kitchen. My eyes are drawn back to the column of ants.

'Kitty used to come up here sometimes in the evenings.' She settles down with her cup and saucer. 'I think Bob liked to spend a lot of time working on his computer. She really was ready to go, though.' She nods sagely. 'She couldn't wait.' The doorbell rings and I look at the time and sigh. I must go and once again am left wondering why Kitty was so desperate to leave.

Then next morning, full of the joys of life, I fail to notice a piece of baggage carelessly left lying in my path and almost land in the willing arms of Khun Pornsak.

'Good morning, madame,' he says silkily, leading me around the offending baggage whilst throwing an angry glare, followed by a few spitting words, to a passing minion. As we go through the usual pleasantries designed to test my Thai, I find myself watching his face avidly, noting his expressions and those melting eyes – Khun Pornsak, unlike most Thai people, has large, Middle-Eastern-like eyes.

Pity he is so short. Still, I could always use the eyes. I ponder this silently then notice he has stopped talking and is waiting for me to speak.

'Sorry?'

'It means thank you and goodbye,' he repeats the phrase. I realise it is new phrase time and follow the usual procedure, hastily stuffing it into my mental filing cabinet as Aroon mercifully arrives to take me to the market.

When we get back to the hotel later, a bellboy appears at the door with a trolley to take the five-gallon bottle of drinking water I have bought. I turn and, suddenly remembering the phrase from that morning, repeat it to Aroon. He gives a little smile – more to himself than me, I think – and then says, 'Goodbye, madame,' before getting back into the car.

Feeling thoroughly pleased with myself, I follow the bellboy to the lift, and when he finally deposits the crate in the kitchen for me, I hand him a tip and repeat the phrase again. The young bellboy looks rather taken aback.

He expected me to say it in English, I tell myself smugly, and smile knowingly to him as he backs out of the kitchen, eyes agog, obviously amazed at my command of the Thai language.

I go down to the coffee shop for lunch, and as usual Lalana, the head waitress, asks me if I have learned any new phrases today. When I repeat my new-found phrase, I sit back smugly. She looks at me with puzzled amusement. 'I love you?'

'You can't be serious!' I stare back, horrified. 'Are you sure?'

'Yes,' she assures me with a wide smile.

'We'll have to get a proper Thai teacher,' I say when Mo gets back from the office.

CHAPTER FIVE

'*Sawadee kha.*' The small but bulbous with baby Thai lady filling the doorway smiles at me and Mo and goes on to speak what to me sounds like utter gibberish.

'Sorry, I don't understand,' I apologise, wondering how on earth someone could be so heavily pregnant and want to take on evening work as well as a day job.

'Come in, please.' I urge her to sit down at the dining table, hoping I haven't picked the wobbly footed cane chair and, if I have, that it will hold out under the strain.

'My name is Ratana. I teach at the university, so I am an *Ah-jahn.*' She sits down and shuffles her body into a comfortable position.

'Um, when is the baby due?' I ask tentatively.

'Oh, a little while yet, but no problem.' Ratana waves any imaginary doubt aside. 'I will only take leave for a very short time because I must go back to work. My mother will look after the baby for me,' she assures me (my mouth is hanging open in a state of shocked disbelief). 'It is the Thai way.'

She is remarkably patient, I think as Mo and I stumble over the incredibly difficult phrases, like a couple of infants.

'You must be very careful how you say a word,' Ratana warns us, 'because the same word can mean many different things, depending on the tone.' Remembering the episode with Aroon and the bellboy, I nod gravely, resolving to watch my tones carefully from now on and not merely to fumble around in my chaotic mental filing system when I want to say something.

The Thai lesson proves to be a thirsty and exhausting experience, so a drink at the pub is called for, we both agree. Just as we are about to leave the phone rings.

I pick up the receiver. 'It's Eva, I've spoken to Tom and I'm afraid you won't be able to come to the talk after all. It's strictly for the company wives.' She sounds apologetic. 'I do think it's stupid, but there you are,' she adds.

'Never mind.' Mo puts his arm around me comfortingly. 'We'll survive, let's go for a drink.'

The sundowners are there as usual, all sitting along one side of the bar. We join them and banter away matily. A young lady appears and walks up to Max, has a brief conversation and then goes away. 'My girlfriend,' Max informs us. 'Although she might not be if she thinks she can lay down the law,' he says, eyes narrowing. Max, it transpires, used to have a Thai wife but is now divorced and lives on his own. Theo starts ribbing him about his girlfriend.

'What about your girlfriend?' Max retaliates.

'Oh?' My ears prick up. 'Why haven't we met her?'

'He wouldn't bring her in here,' Max informs us. 'Frightened he might lose her.'

'She doesn't like to go out,' Theo says matter-of-factly. 'She doesn't drink. Anyway, she's happy to be at home.'

'Doesn't get much choice if you won't bring her.' Max looks straight ahead, sipping his beer.

Theo's eyes turn stormy.

Sensing an argument brewing, I change the subject. 'Are you going to Guy's retiral do?' Guy is retiring from the oil company in a few weeks, and we have been invited to the party. The idea is to get them away from talking about Theo's girlfriend, although I am boiling with curiosity. Max, in a bid to make 'winner of the wooden spoon' award for the evening, manages to bring her back into the conversation.

'Bringing her to the party?'

'As a matter of fact, I am,' Theo announces haughtily, taking a quick draw on his fag. A few beers later, Max informs us that he is employed by the CIA.

Some bigwigs in the army must be having lunch in the coffee shop, I note, judging by the line of expensive cars parked outside the doorway and the unmistakable presence of soldiers dotted around. The muffled sound of the lunchtime singers filters out through the glass doors as I make my way to the lift.

The doors part and Monique emerges. 'Hello,' she says, smiling.

'Oh, Monique. Hi.' I am surprised by her sudden appearance, not to mention her beaming smile.

'I would like to go to the market tomorrow, if that is OK?' Monique says as I get into the lift.

'Yes. Yes, of course.' My reply is rather stilted as my mind does its best to register both Monique's sudden enthusiasm and the fact that I seem to be about to share the lift with two dubious-looking men and a soldier clutching a submachine gun.

'I'm going to buy a chicken,' I hear myself suddenly announcing in the confusion. 'Talk to you later,' I shout as the lift doors begin to close. The rashness of my outburst only hits me when I see Monique staring back at me as if I have gone completely mad. Now I am left alone with this Rambo look-alike and a contingent from the Thai Mafia and fervently wishing we didn't live on the eleventh floor.

The next morning Monique and I pick our way carefully along the now-familiar stretches of concrete that serve as a haphazard form of pavement leading to the street where the market is held.

The sun is already out in force, warming the air and nurturing the various ominous odours that I have long since given up trying to identify. Monique, hair pulled back in a tight bun, walks with a stiffly held, disapproving head, her eyes cast warily downwards. I find myself pulling my shoulders back to match hers. This girl is obviously not programmed to slouch.

The pavements, when they exist, on either side of the road, are lined with market people sitting beside their wares spread out around them, either set out on large leaves on the ground or piled in large, loosely woven baskets. I can't help wondering if any of them have been peed on, but I keep my thoughts to myself.

'I think perhaps we ought to have come earlier,' I say as the street sweeper shoves a pile of dubious-looking rubbish towards our feet. Monique eyes the rubbish and immediately puts on an air of incredulous superiority.

'I forgot, the street market finishes by eight o'clock,' I say, annoyed with myself for having allowed Monique to set the time. When I have walked down this street on other days after eight, there has been no sign of any market having been here at all, which, given Monique's Victorian attitude to the whole expedition, would have been a less fraught introduction. As it is, she has the disapproving air of a missionary in a whorehouse.

Not wanting to run the gauntlet of the fish paste in the alleyway leading to the permanent market, I fix my eye on a chicken stall that is just packing up and march towards it. The woman behind the stall nonchalantly slices the head off one of the two whole chickens that are left and tosses it carelessly to the side. I wince, point to the chicken and ask how much it is.

'Well, that wasn't so bad after all.' I smile, holding the plastic bag up triumphantly. Monique looks too stunned to speak. As we cross the road, the Thai national anthem starts playing and everyone immediately stops what they are doing and stands to attention. Monique and I stand still, me doing my best to ignore the large, mangy dog at my feet, chewing what looks like some animal's innards dusted in a coating of dirt. I fervently hope this festering canine won't take my exposed toes to be part of its meal.

'Why don't we go back and have something to drink?' I ask, relieved to find that my toes are still intact when the music stops at last and everyone is bustling back into action again. Unfortunately, Monique has also spotted the dog and turned that same pale, yellowy colour of the whites after they come out of the washing machine here.

'I'm afraid it will have to be instant in mugs,' I warn Monique when she asks for coffee. I don't want her to experience any further shock when I don't produce the posh matching set she has. The disturbingly warm chicken is now safely chilling in the fridge.

'We haven't got ourselves organised yet,' I call across to where she is sitting on one of the armchairs, looking polite and as unapproachable as ever. The exaggerated dimensions of the room seem to emphasise her loneliness. This girl is not happy.

'So how do you like living here?' I place the mug on the glass-topped coffee table in front of Monique, completely at a loss as to what else to say.

Her gaze drops. 'Oh, it's all right,' she says in a tone that implies it isn't. 'I think perhaps it would be better if we had a house on the compound.' She stares at her mug. 'Sometimes it's very lonely here all day and boring. It's difficult for me because I don't know how things are done and I don't want to make any mistakes. The other ladies know so much.' She picks up her coffee mug and holds it thoughtfully. 'Also, we have only been married for a short time.'

She turns to gaze at me, and I suddenly realise those eyes lack the sparkle of a well-humped newly-wed.

'It all happened so suddenly; there was a phone call to say that Jacques was being posted here. We brought the date of our wedding forward.' She sighs heavily. 'I gave up my job and then everything was postponed. For two months no word.' She shrugs her shoulders. 'Nobody cares. I gave up a very good job and then we didn't know what was happening. It was all so difficult.'

She replaces her coffee mug on the table and sits back with an air of resignation. 'I was always so busy before. Now,' she shrugs her shoulders helplessly and stares at her coffee mug again, 'there is nothing to do here and the company won't let me take a job.'

I can't help feeling sorry for her, and as she is leaving, I tell her to drop in any time for a chat. She kindly offers to lend us a radio and we say we'll get together again, but I'm not sure that will happen; she seems dug in too deeply in her own misery. I wonder what Jacques is like.

Later I remove the chicken from the fridge, smear it with oil and lime juice as I have yet to find any lemons, sprinkle it with salt, stick a few garlic pieces under the skin, and put it into the oven.

'You know, I'm really getting to like it here,' I say chattily as I check the bird cooking in the oven, savouring the aroma of chicken blasting up my nostrils.

'Oh?' Mo is behind me hovering around the welcome smell; I don't think he can quite believe his luck.

'Yes.' I close the oven door with the firmness and confidence of a master chef and shake out the cloth I was using as an oven glove. 'I mean, this apartment's not bad,' I say, matching corners precisely as I fold the cloth and then lay it on the counter, 'and if anything goes wrong, we can just pick up the phone. We're within walking distance, if not always carrying distance of the market, that tiny supermarket place and the post office.' I wipe the knife I have just washed on a towel. 'So, it's really ideal.'

'Apart from the tourists,' Mo says cautiously.

'Oh, the tourists are no problem,' I go on airily.

'Well, they are if you are trying to get the lift at 7am, which seems to be the time the poor sods have to leave for their next destination. Not to mention tripping over their baggage in the reception area, and this is still the rainy season; it will only get worse, I was thinking,' Mo goes on.

'I had coffee with Grace earlier on and she said we were in the best place because living in a house is a bit risky, apparently. According to her Thai friends, there are quite a few break-ins, not to mention power cuts – well you've seen the state of the wiring outside,' I say as I open the fridge door and take out a plate of mixed fruit for Mo. 'It's like spaghetti gone wrong. You also must keep a dog. Rabies can incubate for years, or so I've read.' I hand the fruit to Mo and rummage in the drawer for a fork. 'And it's almost impossible to get things fixed quickly when they break down and, according to a Thai woman that Grace is very friendly with, all sorts of things can happen. So, I suppose we're lucky.' I pick a mug from the cupboard. 'I'll bring your tea in a minute, love.'

When I take the mug of tea to him Mo is all but obliterated by the newspaper. *Hmm, another cosy, chatty evening*, I think wryly. Still, I am feeling proud of my achievement. *The chicken is a small step but nevertheless a significant one*, I tell myself.

Later I remove the precious bundle from the oven. My heart is pounding as I set the dish on the countertop and prepare to carve. Mo, newly showered, is pouring us each a drink.

'God, that smells good,' he breathes behind me. Knife poised, I feel the saliva gathering in my mouth as I carefully begin to slice downwards.

The breast meat comes away beautifully. Breath held and heart thumping, I lift each piece and carefully place it on a specially warmed plate. That done, I throw Mo a smile, take a quick sip from the glass he has put down for me and start on the legs.

Then, as I prise away the first leg, I spot them. 'Shit,' I say viciously, suddenly feeling sick.

'What's wrong?'

'It's still got its fucking feet on.'

Mo eats his, but I can tell he isn't really enjoying it. I can't face mine. I keep seeing those nails, claws or whatever they are called, stuck up its bum. I mean, you never know where it's been and I'm quite sure they don't give every chicken a manicure or use a nailbrush on them.

Plan B, or is it C now? I am going to have to make a real effort with this cooking business.

The next morning Aroon comes to pick me up as usual and I sit in the car as we make our way through the mayhem of traffic. He always drives with the deliberate care one normally reserves for the driving test, much to Mo's annoyance. As we come to a crossroads, he immediately switches on the hazard warning lights, which is supposed to indicate to all the other drivers that he is going straight ahead. I sigh and shake my head; the logic of this is too hysterical to dwell on.

We pass an old woman loping along with two huge baskets suspended like scales from a bar hung over her shoulders. *How on earth can she do that in this heat?* I wonder. My eyes follow the ever-changing scenes outside. It seems that every few yards someone is trying to sell food of one kind or another, which reminds me that I have tonight's dinner to think about. So far everything I have tackled hasn't quite worked. The soup tastes different; in fact, everything does, even the imported goods, which are so horrendously expensive. Maybe it's time to try the local food. Anyone can do a stir-fry and I do have enough vegetables.

'We go buy rice,' I tell Aroon.

Aroon turns and smiles. 'Madame like Thai rice?'

'I hope so, Aroon.' *I really hope so*, I mutter to myself.

Aroon stops the car and parks in the usual place near the main market entrance. He opens the door for me carefully and closes it just as carefully behind me. 'Madame buy rice,' he states again to make sure, and leads the way as I follow on behind carefully, ever-mindful of potential hazards lurking only they and God know where.

He leads me into what seems like a small barn of a place big enough to afford a cooling escape from the heat. I see sacks and sacks of rice piled up around us, all different prices and qualities. I haven't a clue what to ask for. I sift some grains through my fingers from one of the open sacks on display. 'Is this good?'

'Yes, madame, this good,' Aroon assures me.

'Better than this?' I pick up a handful of grains from another sack. 'Or that?' I point to a third sack.

Aroon's face creases into a beaming smile. 'I don know, madame.' He shrugs.

Typical bloody man, I think, throwing him the obligatory smile. *God, why is everything so complicated?* I wonder, silently wishing I could conjure up some hitherto-unthinkable Uncle Ben's.

'One minute, madame,' Aroon says, and turns to chat to a well-fed-looking man sitting beside a till, diligently picking his nose. After a long conversation, which leaves me lost, and seriously thinking baked potatoes, no matter what the marital consequences, Aroon finally grins to the man and then turns towards a sack behind them. 'This number one, madame,' he says confidently.

'OK, OK. A kilo, please,' I say quickly, relieved to be able to make a decision at last.

'Now I need to buy a box,' I tell Aroon. Yesterday I came across some ants in the cupboard, tripping daintily out from an expensive packet of almonds, like ladies leaving a posh restaurant in high heels. No way are they having my newly acquired rice.

A shophouse, packed with hardware items stashed in every available corner and the rest dangling precariously above our heads, eventually produces a large plastic bowl with a lid, so I buy it. When we get back to the hotel I wash the bowl, dry it carefully and pour the rice into it immediately, pressing the lid closed defiantly. *That'll keep the buggers out*, I tell myself, and go off for a much-needed shower to cool off before I have coffee with Grace.

Time for yet another Thai lesson, and I am sitting with my head bowed over the column of incomprehensible words in front of me as Ratana reads out the proper pronunciation. I am listening with only one ear because I am on my own wondering where the hell Mo has got to; he is late again, and I am raging inside. *He could at least make the effort*, I think, and then realise with a sinking feeling that I have just missed how to pronounce half the column.

'Now you repeat, please?' Ratana's eyes gaze at me enquiringly over the width of the dining-room table.

'Em,' I sigh and resign myself, then jump as the door bursts open.

'Sorry I'm late,' Mo dashes past. 'Be there in a minute.'

I should bloody well hope so, I voice silently, throwing him a look that displays my thoughts. 'I am sorry,' I tell Ratana.

'Never mind.' She smiles with the tranquil air of late-stage pregnancy. 'Khun Mo is very busy working.'

I am highly relieved when Mo finally sits down beside me. However, to add insult to injury, when he doesn't know the proper tone, he tries all of them and adds another word that sounds like the Thai word in an effort to lighten the atmosphere. For some reason she gives us the word for pants and Mo says something that rhymes with the Thai word. I am busy sending him threatening glances when the table, never stable at the best of times, starts to tremble.

I immediately think, *earthquake*, and glance at Mo, who is obviously thinking along the same lines, then we both turn to look at Ratana, who is doubled up, clutching her stomach and shaking with a grimace on her face.

Oh, hell, I think, and then wonder how to say 'there's a pregnant lady giving birth on the eleventh floor' in Thai. This is quickly followed by a vision of the entire reception staff equally doubled up at my attempts to say it.

I flash a 'what do we do now?' look at Mo, who stares back, wide-eyed. He shrugs his shoulders, gorilla-fashion. The faint noise of the traffic filtering in from outside seems to emphasise our isolation.

Oh God, Ratana's body is trembling with a force that would have registered at least five on the Richter scale. This is bound to start her off. I have a vision of the poor baby inside clutching on to the umbilical cord for dear life, head bouncing off the placenta. Any baby with an ounce of sense would bale out. I look back at Mo, who is staring in incredulous wonder.

'Oh.' Ratana lets out a gasp. I tense and widen my eyes in horror as Ratana's head bends down under the table.

Oh God, she's going to have it on the floor. I panic and start to get out of my chair, furiously trying to dig out an article from my mind I had once read about what to do if a woman starts to give birth and you can't get to hospital. I am guiltily aware that I opted out at the bit about how to cut the cord.

I throw Mo a look of panic, then follow his eyes across the table as Ratana surfaces again, her hand clutching a paper tissue. 'So sorry,' she gasps, and sniffs noisily. I slump back with relief. 'But Khun Mo said a very rude word.' She sniffs again, patting the tears from her cheeks.

'Really?' I'm hanging on to her every word.

Ratana sits back and takes a deep breath. 'That word only men use for women's private parts.'

'Mo,' I hiss, trying not to laugh. 'In future if you don't know just say so.'

'You must be careful,' Ratana goes on. 'Different tone has a different meaning.' She blinks and the chair creaks as she sits back, more composed now. My shoulders sink with relief.

'Like word for bananas,' she continues, watching us both soberly.

'Bananas?' I feel myself tense and warily take a sip of water.

'Yes, word for bananas. If you say wrong way, it is same as rude word for man's penis.'

Mouth opens in horror; I look across at Mo. 'Well, don't expect me to walk around the market with you in future,' he quips, barely able to suppress his amusement.

When Ratana leaves, I tackle Mo about his timekeeping. 'Why can't you manage to arrive on time? You were the one who set the time, and anyway, you're supposed to finish at four-thirty. I mean, being late's bad enough, but you can't even remember the words,' I tell him as I carefully remove the large plastic bowl containing the rice I bought the other day from the cupboard.

'Look, it may have escaped your notice,' Mo plops ice cubes into a glass with the emphasis of one whose patience is being severely tried, 'but when I leave this apartment every morning, having endured a cold shower because the bloody tourists have used up all the hot water, not to mention risking life and limb climbing over an array of baggage that makes an army assault course look like a stroll through the park,' he pauses for breath and unscrews the cap from the gin bottle, 'I go to work. Not,' he goes on, 'to spend all day in an air-conditioned office.'

I watch defiantly as he pours a dubious measure of gin over the ice. 'I have to go out to the oil field where it's bloody hot and the sweat pours out of me in pints. I've given up counting the number of showers I have in a day.' He bangs down the gin bottle and begins to screw the cap on.

'You have no idea what it's like,' he goes on, opening the fridge door and removing a bottle of tonic. 'I go back to the office and find that my secretary doesn't seem to be able to type anything in English without making a complete arse of it, so I have to spend the next three hours sorting that out.' He fills what is left of the space in the glass with some tonic.

'I get hot too, you know,' I say in high dudgeon, gripping the plastic lid with my nails, 'and you don't have to go to the bloody – and I use the word advisedly – market every day, watching poor, defenceless creatures being tortured to death,' I fume, wrenching at the plastic.

'I've already told you; you just have to get used to it and that's that.'

I tug at the lid and peel it back slowly.

'I try to get back as soon as I can,' Mo begins again, and then stops as he realises I am staring at the rice in horror.

'Bugger!' I slam the useless bloody lid to the floor.

'Now what's wrong?' Mo says, peering into the bowl. The rice inside is heaving gently as a mass of tiny heads and bodies of varying descriptions waver around in surprise at the sudden light.

'We'll eat downstairs tonight,' he says quickly.

'I can't understand it.' I am close to tears now, chin quivering. 'I bought that bowl with the lid specially so that nothing could get into the damned rice.' I sigh.

'They didn't get in; they were already there, or at least the eggs were. You just provided the ideal condition for them to hatch out, that's all,' he tries to placate me.

I throw up my hands in horror. 'A whole kilo of rice!'

'It's hardly going to break the bank.'

'That's not the point.'

'Look, weevils are a fact of life; they get into all kinds of foodstuffs, not only rice and not just here. You get them in the UK.'

'Well, I haven't seen any.'

'I told you: you gave them the right conditions to hatch out,' he says, emphasising every word.

'Well, thanks for the biology lesson; from now on I'm keeping everything in the fridge,' I tell him. 'That way the buggers will freeze to death.'

CHAPTER SIX

Cookie appears in the pub one evening. Her guests have gone now, and we arrange to meet the next day so that she can show me around. She takes me to the big *Wat* (temple). Carefully removing our shoes, we venture inside, relieved to get away from the stifling heat, and I stare in wonder at the huge golden effigy of Buddha; it is indeed beautiful. People are milling around everywhere, monks in saffron-coloured robes sit chanting, with eyes closed, and some grinning pigs' heads are lined up on one side each with a flower stuck in its ear. I find this even more surreal than the scene at the market. A rattling sound comes from a group of women kneeling, intent on shaking what look to be like spills in tall beakers. It is some kind of fortune-telling, Cookie tells me. And all the time the huge Buddha sits quietly, above all of this, cross-legged, one hand resting upwards on his lap whilst the other rests over his right leg displaying four, exceptionally long, even-length fingers.

Cookie has been trying to find out everything she can about Buddhism here: a subject that fascinates her. We follow the story of Buddhism told in pictures on the wall beside the main doors, which are inlaid with mother-of-pearl. The workmanship is amazing and according to the guidebook took 'five months and twenty days to complete'.

Eventually we wander reluctantly into the heat outside and around the huge grounds. There is so much to see, and I notice stalls selling packaged foodstuffs for visitors to take back with them, as well as souvenirs and clothes. Away from the main building is a gigantic statue of a standing Buddha and beside it a place where the novice monks are sitting talking. It also has a small zoo with, amongst other things, a monkey that smokes cigarettes as a party piece. We walk for as long as we can bear the heat, before making our way back.

Cookie has one more *Wat* she wants me to see, across the road from the hotel. This *Wat* is much smaller and more humbly adorned but nevertheless a beautiful, peaceful sanctuary. We climb the steps and venture inside, walking carefully over the highly polished, dark wooden floor, and sit down for a moment. A young monk appears and begins talking to us; he seems keen to practise his stilted English and we are happy to oblige. When he finally runs out of things to say, he excuses himself and leaves. We sit for a while savouring the cool silence before we go.

Outside and across the road, we meet two women dressed in white robes. According to Cookie this is the closest a woman can get to becoming a monk. Their faces break into huge smiles as they spot her. They cannot speak much English, but the message is clear: they absolutely adore her.

'Personally, I do not care to stay on the compound,' Cookie remarks a while later as she prepares two mugs of coffee in her tiny kitchen. *This is much more my style*, I think, relief flowing through me. I can relax here, and it's the same when I go to visit Grace.

We move through to the lounge area. This apartment, I note, is the same as Monique's, with the obligatory life-size monk meditating in the corner. I find myself wondering if this is an indication of the woman's taste or a standard company decoration.

'There is too much sniping amongst the women,' Cookie says, as she places her mug on the glass-topped coffee table, 'and everyone knows your business. They make all these rules and regulations about the compound and then they fall out about them. Which way the traffic should go around the roundabout, what time the club should close; they even spend their time moaning because they haven't got a squash court.' She throws up her hands in despair. 'These women are bored; they have nothing to do all day, so they start bitching.' She proffers a plate of biscuits.

I shake my head. 'No, thanks.'

'They should find something interesting to do. Me, I want to know about the Buddhists. So.' She picks up a biscuit and begins to gesticulate. I listen intently, shifting my body to a more comfortable position on the rattan couch. 'I go and find out everything I can about them,' Cookie continues, finally taking a bite of her biscuit.

A loud, whooping noise breaks into the silence as Cookie chews her biscuit.

'What is that noise? I keep hearing it; it sounds awful.' I wince, getting up and moving towards the balcony window.

'It's a monkey, a gibbon,' Cookie says, following behind me. 'It belongs to the man across the road.' She opens the balcony doors, letting the traffic noise crash in. 'He keeps it in that cage outside,' she says, pointing. 'Apparently every time the maid goes to the market it gets lonely, so it starts to make a noise.'

'I'll take your word for it,' I tell her, declining to look and backing off from the balcony.

'All the expats in the hotel were going to club together to buy it and set it free, but the owner won't part with it. Sometimes it drives me crazy, and I just have to go out.' Cookie sighs heavily and closes the balcony doors. 'I will show you around,' she says when we are sitting down again. 'You should meet the ladies. I'll take you to the compound. They do patchwork sewing on a Thursday.' She smiles encouragingly.

'But I don't do patchwork,' I say hastily, not sure that I like the idea.

'No matter,' Cookie assures me. 'You should meet the ladies.'

'I'm not sure that this is a good idea,' I tell Mo the next morning, 'but in the interests of being sociable, I'll go.'

The compound is much smaller than I imagined, and I am highly relieved to have got here at all. Cookie's driving is something akin to Cruella de Vil going after her Dalmatian skin coat.

'You know, to begin with I was terrified of driving here, but,' she took her hand off the wheel to gesticulate, 'I told myself, Cookie, you just have to do it or be a prisoner in that hotel.' Now she drives like a woman possessed. Then turning into the compound, we almost collide with another car.

'Idiot!' she shrieks, shaking her fist at the chalk-faced man we have almost collided with head-on.

She turns her blazing eyes on me. 'Did you see that? That idiot almost killed us – he was driving on the wrong side of the road!'

'Actually, Cookie, he was on the proper side; they drive on the left-hand side of the road, same as in the UK.' I feel relieved at last to be able to point out.

Those still-blazing eyes stare at me for a few seconds before it sinks in. 'You know?' She slaps her hand on the wheel. 'You are right, so they do. But he was going too fast.' My attempt to stifle a laugh at this point ends up in a fit of coughing that brings mascara-threatening tears to my eyes.

When we are past the security guards, I crane my neck to take in every detail of this relative paradise with its large houses set in manicured gardens, decked in splashes of colourful bushes and trees. 'Oh, just look at that,' I whisper as I catch sight of the huge blue swimming pool fringed with palm trees and empty sun loungers. It's like driving into an oasis in the middle of the desert, a whole world away from the poverty, dust and mayhem outside. If I could live in a place like this, I'd be in seventh heaven. No wonder Monique is upset.

'This is it,' Cookie announces, pulling on the handbrake. I feel my stomach tense as I get out of the car and follow her up the path to one of a row of three identical houses.

'Oh, hello.' It's Frances who greets us. 'You'll never guess what's happened,' she launches. 'I'm absolutely furious,' she goes on. 'A certain person,' she nods her head knowingly as we quickly remove our shoes, 'has cancelled all weekend leave.' She stares at Cookie, her eyes wide with anger.

'No. Really?'

Frances lifts an eyebrow by way of reply.

We stand whilst Frances continues her diatribe. I am hastily acknowledged and shiver as we all move into the body of the room. The AC is fierce. I catch sight of Eva sitting, or rather perched on the far corner of a large cane sofa. Monique has settled herself rather unhappily, I can't help thinking, in a pupil position on a low pouffe across from Eva's feet, her face devoid of any telling expression. I find myself scanning the room for the monk by way of support. Mercifully two other women arrive, which means that the whole diatribe is repeated and then the wife of the accused walks in to join the party.

'Your husband is not popular,' she is told by way of a greeting, and from that moment I wish I could simply go home.

The other women sit, dotted around the generously proportioned room, bare feet settled on the marble floor, primly attacking their patches of cloth, each woman silently hugging her fury.

The atmosphere is saturated with resentment; once we are all seated, polite words of exchange are batted back and forth like a slow tennis game. *There is no room for friendship or easy laughter here*, I decide, wondering why we are freezing our knickers off inside when a perfectly good sun is shining obligingly outside, not to mention a swimming pool to die for. I throw Cookie a 'let's get out of here' look that somehow gets lost in the translation.

'Frances, do you still have that book about Thailand?' Cookie asks instead.

'I think so.' Frances puts aside her patchwork and scans her bookshelves. Finally, she picks out a large coffee-table-style tome.

'It's really interesting, you'll like it,' Cookie says, wide-eyed and nodding to me as she passes it over. Smouldering inside, I raise one eyebrow, politely accept the book with a sinking heart and proceed to look through the pictures, nursing my own silent fury.

Halfway through the book I sneak another glance around the room. Eva is flapping the front of her blouse about. 'Is it just me or does anyone else find it hot in here?'

Give me strength, I plead silently, and glare meaningfully across at Cookie, who, eyes down, is sewing with astounding diligence.

'This place is really getting me down,' Frances slices into the silence. 'There's absolutely nothing to do here. I mean, once you've seen one *Wat*, you've seen them all.'

'Oh, I don't know.' I feel compelled to speak, with the air of an enthusiastic rookie. 'They are all different,' I point out, remembering my sojourn with Cookie.

'After four years they all look the same, I can tell you,' Frances says in a voice that brooks no argument. 'So, what do you think of this place?' Frances's eyes flick briefly in my direction.

'I like it,' I say, taken aback by this sudden attention, then realise that this is not the prescribed response. I have just dropped a boulder from a bloody great height and completely squashed any further conversation.

A threatening silence ensues. Thoroughly fed up now, I throw a third penetrating glance at Cookie, leaving her in no doubt that if we don't leave now, I won't be responsible for my actions.

'Don't ever do that to me again. Please,' I tell her as we walk back towards the car. 'From now on I'm steering clear of anything to do with these women unless I absolutely have to.'

'They are very upset, but no, you are right, they were not very friendly.'

'I'm sure they must be very upset,' I say as the car sweeps past the tennis courts. I can't help thinking of the austere apartment we have compared to these grand houses, not to mention being able to order food up from Bangkok on a regular basis. Compared to the rest of us these people are pampered and well provided for; they live in a different world.

'So, this is what Monique wants?'

'Yes, but in her case, it won't make her any happier when she gets here. It's about belonging,' Cookie says. 'She feels excluded amongst other things,' she adds ominously. 'Look at what they did to me. The manager had a lunch for all the ladies and didn't invite me. I'm pretty tough, but I felt bad about it; even though I don't want to live with them, I am still part of the same company. When you are out on your own you are vulnerable.'

When I see her next for a coffee, Cookie says, 'I must just finish preparing our meal for later.' She lifts the lid of a pot to reveal a beef stew with vegetables that Mo would love. The beef from the market I have been warned is tough and not worth buying unless you can get the fillet.

I have now solved the rice problem by keeping it in the fridge and graduated to chicken breasts and pork fillet, which I stir-fry every which way, using the recipes from the Thai cookery book I bought with some of the money, which was my leaving present from my friends and colleagues at the college. These two kinds of meat are to be our staple for the next four years. If I spot the live chickens tied together by their feet in a bunch under the stall, we have pork. If I hear the pigs being slaughtered – a long, drawn-out, nerve-shattering experience – we have chicken. If I encounter both in the same day we have stir-fried veg or go out.

Cookie finishes preparing the stew and we sit down to have coffee. I discover that she likes to paint but hasn't done so for a while and also plays the classical flute, but again has not played for some time. 'I will again soon, but I have to be in the mood, and it can be so depressing when you are on your own.' She often goes down to the pub early in the evening and has a drink and a chat with the sundowners. 'Otherwise, I would go mad,' she tells me. 'It's hard being on your own in a strange country, but to be with the other women all of the time listening to all their complaints. No, thank you. I'd rather be here.' She lights a cigarette and blows the smoke out thoughtfully. 'But you know, sometimes I am frightened being here alone; I keep thinking what if someone knows I am on my own and tries to break into the apartment?'

The sound of the gibbon whooping across the road has us across at the balcony. Cookie opens the doors, letting in the roar of the traffic. I retreat to the sofa. She closes the doors again. 'You know, I got really upset one time. There was a man exposing himself at me from that building across the street.'

'No. Honestly?' I'm riveted on the sofa, waiting for the rest.

'Yeah. He knew that every so often I go and look out over the balcony, and he would open his pants. I was disgusted, terrified that he would find my room and arrive at my door. Twice I called reception to complain, but each time when they got here, he had gone. They didn't believe me.'

'So, what did you do?'

'Well, the third time it happened I went down to reception and got Bonchai, the young assistant manager. I told him, "You must come now; you must come now," and made him come back up to the room with me.'

'And was the man still there?'

'No, he had gone, but this time I wasn't giving in. I told Bonchai that the man was exposing himself. I pointed to the balcony and said, "Look out there, look at the green-roofed house. That man is exposing himself."'

I suddenly realise my mouth is hanging open and quickly clamp it shut. 'What did he say?'

'Well, it was obvious from the look on his face that he hadn't a clue what I was talking about. So, I had to demonstrate.' She stubs out her cigarette and stands up. 'I told him the man was pulling his trousers down. Trousers, pants, he was pulling them down,' she says, pulling at her own trousers to demonstrate as she speaks. 'I looked him straight in the eye, pointed to his trousers and kept pulling at my own, saying very slowly, "He was taking his trousers down, trousers, pants, taking them down."' She carries on demonstrating.

I am wiping the tears from my eyes now. 'Did he get the message?'

'No! He stood there looking at me like a dead fish, staring eyes, mouth wide open, and then he started to giggle. I think he thought I wanted him to take his trousers down. The more I tried to tell him and show him the more he giggled and then he backed out of the door, still giggling. I tell you, I was mad as hell.'

'Oh, Cookie, the poor guy must have thought that this forty-year-old woman whose husband was away had brought him up to her room to seduce him.' By this time, we are both in tears laughing.

'And now every time he sees me, he just giggles,' she says, sitting down again. 'But the next time it happened, Khun Pornsak and a few other men went across to the man's house – I don't know what happened, but when they got back Pornsak's hand was bleeding.'

That evening Mo and I discover that a swarm of bees have decided to take up residence on one of the flowering bushes on the middle balcony. We are both pleased to see them, and I hope they will stay. They are still there the next morning when Cookie calls.

'You have what on your balcony?'

'Bees, Cookie, bees.' I look across at the mass of insects clinging to the branch of the corner bush. 'A whole swarm of them,' I announce like a proud mother hen clucking over her brood.

'I'm coming to see.'

A few minutes later she is standing at the door. 'Where are they?' Her eyes are wide with anticipation.

I lead her across to the balcony and quietly open the door to let her have a better view. 'Isn't it great? Aren't they lovely?' I tilt my head dotingly.

'Oh yes.' Cookie's eyes and lips widen simultaneously, head nodding slowly the way people do when they're not quite sure if they are dealing with a lunatic.

'Perhaps they are resting, no?'

'Oh. I hope not,' I say, horrified at the very thought. 'I want them to stay.'

'You want them to stay.' Cookie is looking deep into my eyes, her head doing an imitation of a mechanical nodding donkey.

'Yes. I just want to have something alive around again. I miss talking to my cat. I miss the company.' I let out a deep sigh.

Cookie's eyes are staring back at me with the horrified caution of one who has realised she is talking to a lunatic and had better tread carefully.

'We used to keep bees, Cookie. We had our own beehives.'

'Ah.' The relief is obvious.

'The only thing that worries me is that the maid might have them taken away.'

A few minutes later, as if on cue, Kik arrives to clean. When she spots the bees she says, 'Oh,' the way East Asians do, and makes off to fetch the caretaker.

'No. No!' We call her back and try to explain that I want to keep the bees, but no amount of gesticulating and pleading will do. She doesn't understand.

'We have to go down and tell Khun Pornsak, so they do not take them away,' Cookie says.

As we stop in front of the reception desk Bonchai looks up from what he is doing, spots Cookie and immediately starts to giggle. The few other bodies mooning around the reception desk turn to stare.

Cookie's glare is as sharp as an ice pick.

Suppressing an overwhelming desire to join in the merriment, I press my lips together tightly and clear my throat. 'Eh, we have some bees on the balcony,' I begin soberly, watching carefully as Bonchai's eyes become large and blank, his face a study of total incomprehension.

'Bees,' I begin again. 'We have bees.'

Bonchai is frowning now. 'You know, they go *bzzzz*,' I say, and begin flapping my arms for effect. Bonchai's eyes widen with disbelief and everyone else looks away quickly, apart from Cookie, whose face is a study in suppressed amusement.

'Bees. Um.' I flap my hand around for inspiration. 'You know, insects, same insects. You know?'

'Oh, you have insects on your balcony.' His face forms a suitably horrified expression. '*Oooh*. I tell housekeeping to take away.'

'No! No!' I stop flapping and shake my head vigorously. 'I want to keep the bees,' I emphasise. 'I like the insects.' I nod for effect and, like a trouper, Cookie is nodding with me.

He blinks slowly, his features a diplomatic blank. 'You want to keep the insects?'

'Yes,' I sigh, my shoulders sag with relief.

'OK.'

Cookie nudges my elbow. 'Now he thinks we are both mad.'

Kik comes in briskly later. She points in the direction of the bees. 'You like?' Her eyebrows, I notice, are raised disapprovingly.

I am desperate for a swim, so Cookie invites me to go with her to the pool at the compound. Somewhere in the arrangements was a verbal agreement that Mo and I could use this pool, but Theo has warned me against it. 'If you take my advice, you'll stay away from it. Don't have anything to do with it,' was all he would say. But Cookie is adamant, and as I am going as her guest, it seems churlish to refuse.

I needn't have worried: we have the whole pool to ourselves. In fact, I have the whole pool to myself. Cookie is a lifelong sunbather with what she describes as elephant-hide skin to prove it. Her idea of going to the pool is just that. Every so often, and not that often, she gets up and wades into the pool at waist height, where she stands splashing water over her body until she feels sufficiently cooled off, then she wades back out again to resume her bathing in the sun.

On our second visit to the pool, Eva walks past the fence carrying a bundle of loaves of French bread. She calls Cookie over and I amble across with her. 'Just got these,' she says. 'Had to order a batch. Would you like a couple?' Her question is definitely directed at Cookie.

'Oh yes, thank you.' Cookie nods her head.

'Well, come round to the house when you are ready, and you can collect them.'

'OK.' Cookie says, and we amble back to collect our things.

Later we walk over to Eva's house. She holds the door open, and we walk into the kitchen. During the whole time we are in the house, her full attention is directed at Cookie. She is focussed on complaining about a function they are all expected to attend. It's going to be their anniversary, so she doesn't see why she and Tom should have to go. I listen quietly, thankful that I don't have to get caught up in all these problems.

CHAPTER SEVEN

Our R&R weekend is coming up and we decide to go to Chiang Mai, Thailand's second city in the north. This entails Mo trying to get away as early as possible in the afternoon so that we don't end up driving through the mountains after dark. We are armed only with instructions from Mo's predecessor, and we fervently hope that they prove to be more detailed than the instructions he left for using the computer.

I am conscious of our food supply, a pile of bananas, speedily ripening on the back seat. Yesterday I went to the market with Aroon, so we ended up at his friend's stall. I picked up a bunch of bananas to inspect them and luckily (or so I thought) a whole lot dropped off, leaving me with the few that I needed. I handed them to Aroon's friend, who put them in a bag and then, much to my dismay, scooped up the fallen bananas and threw those in too. Aroon took the bag from his friend, poked his head inside, grinned, and said, 'Boss like bananas, madame?' I wondered if word had got round.

Just as we were leaving, I suddenly spotted the bananas on the countertop. They were now going black and to leave them was an open invitation to every mouse, ant and cockroach in the country. The maids weren't around so I stuffed them into the only bag I had, which unfortunately was clear plastic, hoping Mo wouldn't notice.

'Eh, would you like a banana?' I venture, having worked out how many we will have to eat to finish them on the way up without sickening ourselves. It would be better to start now.

'Later,' he says. 'When we get on the road.' At this point he turns round to look out the back window. 'Bloody hell! What on earth possessed you to bring all these bananas?' I explain. He shakes his head.

The roads are surprisingly good, but we constantly must watch out for dogs running out in front of the car or sleeping on the road or at the roadside, seemingly oblivious to the passing traffic. These poor animals are in a terrible state with obvious skin diseases as well as being infested with fleas, judging by the amount of scratching going on. The cats are not much better.

We pass houses hiding amongst tired trees with dust-covered, mottled brown leaves. Some houses are on stilts, providing shade from the sun during the day and cool shelter inside at night. The old teak houses are brown and built near water to keep cool, but the new houses are brightly painted, and many are built with no space underneath.

Hens and cockerels prance around at the roadside, oblivious to any danger, and we see those beautiful, creamy, long-lashed, dirt-spattered cows, plodding along one behind the other in a dubious line. They have a worrying habit of stepping intermittently on and off the tarmac, so Mo gives them a wide berth just in case.

Farmers are fishing in the patchwork of rice fields. A buffalo is wallowing in a ditch at the side. We also see two of them pulling a huge cart, a much more romantic scene than the 'iron buffalo', as the machine is called, which is gradually taking its place. It's an ugly contraption that serves as a tractor, and when the rubber wheels are taken off it becomes a plough for the fields. Unfortunately, according to one of the VSO guys we met in the pub, what once seemed like a good idea is proving to be a costly problem for some farmers when they discover that this magic machine eventually needs spare parts, which must be paid for. The traditional cartwheels are now sadly more commonly used to adorn gates, fences and houses.

Clothes are strung out between trees to dry. Stalls are set up at the roadside selling fruit. A working elephant is plodding home with its keeper. There's so much to take in. As we get nearer the mountains our instructions warn us to beware of high-speed buses. No mention is made of the fact that lorries and buses are oblivious to white lines and that all drivers only try to pass on bends, coming up to bridges and when something is approaching at high speed from the other direction. The Thai nature seems to be that these gentle, smiling men and women turn into demons when they get behind a wheel; the men's macho image will not allow them to give way to anything. I wonder if there's any such thing as a driving test.

A great deal of time on my part is spent hiding behind the instructions as opposed to reading them, as each driver that passes gives us cause to believe we might never reach our destination in one piece, if at all. Each time we are convinced we are about to witness a head-on collision, somehow, miraculously, the two cars manage to pass each other with inches to spare. This journey is not for the faint-hearted.

The mountain roads are indeed steep, and we discover yet another nightmare-inducing situation, that of the overloaded truck. I mean where the load is actually bigger than the truck itself. To be stuck behind one of these going up a steep hill, we might as well get out and walk; it's even worse when smoke is belching from the back. To pass is to invite a collision with a high-speed bus. The journey is fraught with stress.

I am now worried about being hijacked in the dark, another apparent cause for concern. I am wondering whether to take my rings off and put them in my bag or risk having my fingers cut off by some marauding mountain bandits. I wish we hadn't gone to the pub last night; people always have a story to tell that you don't want to hear when they find out that you are about to embark on a journey.

Amazingly we do arrive in one piece, albeit after dark. The lorries, by this time, are decked out with more lights than a Christmas tree. We manage to find our hotel and book in. I'm comforted by a photograph on the wall showing that Princess Diana has stayed here or at least paid a visit.

After a welcome shower and change of clothes, we have something to eat in the coffee shop downstairs and then join a party of Americans on the hotel minibus, which takes us to the infamous night market. The conversations going on around us are about houses and what kind of cars everyone has.

We spend the next couple of hours wandering around, marvelling at Rolex watches sporting plastic straps stamped with the words 'genuine leather'. Gucci, Louis Vuitton, all the big-name handbags, belts, shoes and clothes are here. These are counterfeits, of course, and no one buying them could ever afford the real thing anyway, so it seems like harmless fun that provides a lot of people with jobs. I buy a new handbag and Mo a couple of sports shirts. We also buy some wooden puzzles.

Later we join the minibus and the same Americans and hear all about the purchases and one couple who plan to visit the UK next. They think they might do London in the morning and Edinburgh in the afternoon. Back in our room we go through our purchases and can't resist trying one of the puzzles. Only trouble is we can't put it back together again and there are no instructions. Next morning, we head off up the hill, following the steep, hairpin climb to Wat Prathat Doi Suthep at the top. It is described as stunningly perched on a mountain peak. Legend has it that a white elephant was set off to walk up the mountain and wherever it stopped was to be the sight of the new *Wat*. This was obviously an animal with ambition and a head for heights.

We park the car in the car park and make our way up the road. Mo turns his collar up and I wish I had one. The sun is burning the back of my neck. Halfway up we come to a small funicular railway taking people up to the *Wat* at the top of the hill. 'This is obviously the quickest way to the top,' Mo points out, but I'm not keen; it's a bit steep for me and I have visions of something snapping and the carriage crashing back down again.

We walk on up and come upon some steps flanked by what look to be two seven-headed snarling dragons standing guard, their tails undulating all the way up on either side of the steps. Two hundred and ninety of them, according to the guidebook.

This isn't as steep as the railway, but in the blazing heat it seems a long way up. Finally, I pluck up the courage and we take the railway, although, when we reach the top, I'm not sure my stomach came with me.

Despite the beating sun, people are milling around everywhere and there is a spectacular view of Chang Mai from the top. Huge bells hang in a row with a sign in both Thai and English urging people not to shake the bell. I'm not sure what this means as almost everyone who passes seems hell bent on giving them all a good clang.

Many people are also standing in line, and it seems that they are giving money to a man who pours some liquid into a cup that is then sent up via a small, red-painted dragon on a pulley contraption to be poured out when it reaches the top. We haven't a clue what's going on but join the queue and do it anyway. A small bell jingles as the dragon and cup struggle to the top. I take some photos and then we make our way back down to the road via the steps. A couple of hill tribe children in their native costumes are strategically placed near the bottom of the steps ready to have their photos taken. We notice a man hovering nearby, obviously waiting to collect the money.

Mo's cousin Bea is coming to see us, so we spend the rest of our time sussing out the most interesting things to do.

Chiang Mai is supposed to be one of the world's largest centres of cottage industries. It really is a shopper's paradise, and we eventually find a road outside town that we have been told about, where all the tourist buses go.

All along this road are large shops, factories and their showrooms. We are spoilt for choice: furniture places where you can order whatever you want to be made, shops selling the infamous celadon pottery in blue or green, and intricately designed silver. We watch paper umbrellas being painted by hand in beautiful designs at a place called Bo Sang and fall in love with wood carvings of animals – my favourite. I buy a painted wooden frog lying fast asleep on its back under the shade of a large wooden lily leaf.

We then find the silk factory and spend over an hour wandering around. It has a display showing the whole process of production from the silkworms and their cocoons, ladies spinning the silk, and then an army of girls sitting at looms weaving the silk itself. Finally, we find a shop selling the silk in bolts or made up into an array of garments.

The next place is a factory making pottery. Again, we watch, fascinated, as the designs are all hand-painted on. They also make lacquerware in the same building, and we come across several girls painstakingly picking up minute pieces of eggshell and gluing them on in their natural colours to make a design. It's all so different from the mechanised Western world we come from and humbling to watch. You can't help but appreciate the wonderful skills these people have, which allow them to make their living.

That evening we go back to the night market to hunt out the stall where we bought the puzzles and sheepishly hand the bits of wood over to the man behind the stall. He puts it together in seconds, hands it back and thrusts a piece of paper at us with the solution, for which we are most humbly grateful.

The next morning, we visit an orchid farm. I hadn't realised these plants grow suspended in the air. We wander around admiring the different colours and are given a free orchid to pin on our shirts as we leave. There's also a butterfly farm here and for the first time ever we can watch a beautiful butterfly emerge from its pupae, dry its wings in the sun and then fly off.

The journey back to Pits is equally nail-biting. Every vehicle seems to be stuffed to capacity, whether it be carrying goods or people. At one point we pass an empty bus lying on its side and can only hope everyone got out alive.

My hair badly needs cutting and Grace and Beth suggest that I try a hairdressing school not far from the hotel. Apparently, the owner can speak English.

Feeling a bit apprehensive, I walk in through the open door and see a line of girls seated at the side. A man is sitting at a desk at the other end of the room, and he looks up as I walk in. I smile at the girls, who are all staring at me, nudging each other and stifling giggles.

'Please take a seat,' the rather hunky but ageing salon owner urges me, and points towards a chair in front of his desk.

'I'd like my hair cut, please,' I say doubtfully, clutching my handbag for comfort, fully aware that I am the sole object of attention in the place and the hub of all the giggling going on. 'I'd like a layered cut,' I try to explain.

'*Mai mee pan ha*,' he says, shaking his head. 'That means no problem,' he adds helpfully. This, I have been in Thailand long enough to discover, also translates more often as, 'I don't understand what you are talking about but I'm not going to admit that to you, so I'll say yes and do it anyway.' I can come back tomorrow, he says, at ten o'clock.

The next morning, when I go back, the girls are all sitting in line, but there's no sign of the hairdresser. The giggling begins and the girls invite me to sit down with them. I am once again the sole object of attention as they stare into my face and make comments to each other that I don't understand, which, I tell myself, is probably just as well. A few minutes later a heavily made-up person with a model figure and strangely deep voice suddenly appears and begins prancing around in front of us, in a tight-fitting frock. I am trying to decide whether this person is male or female.

'*Katoy*,' the girls keep saying, giggling and pointing to this person.

Finally, the hairdresser arrives. '*Katoy*,' he says, noticing my bewilderment. 'Boy, girl.' He smiles. 'You wan I cut yoah hay?'

One of the girls takes me through to an area at the back where I see what look to be two massage tables, each one in front of a sink. She indicates that I should lie down and then begins to wash my hair. This is wonderful, so much better than the neck-torturing seats at home. The shampoo is slowly and carefully massaged into my scalp, then my hair is puffed and pounded, before being rinsed thoroughly and then washed again. Once she is finished, I am taken back through to the cutting room.

I sit down gingerly and explain again what I want. 'Ah, same Princess Diana,' he declares. I haven't read an up-to-date UK paper or watched TV for weeks and am frantically trying to remember what her hair is like these days. 'I know. I know,' he says, and begins.

The result is shorter than I really wanted it to be, but the style is more or less right, so I heave a sigh of relief, tell him it is good, pay him the money and walk out into the street, acutely conscious of my newly threshed 'hay'.

The 'beehive' is getting bigger every day, and when M in Bangkok hears about it, he tells us it's lucky, so I hope they don't fly off. Cookie comes up to inspect them and the poor gibbon starts its whooping again.

'At least I won't have to listen to that much longer,' she says cryptically, following me through to the kitchen.

I lift the kettle to pour hot water into the mugs. 'Are you moving to the compound?'

'No, Monique is moving to the compound. We have a new posting.'

'Oh.' I feel the kettle going wobbly and my stomach deflates. I avoid looking at Cookie as I hand her the mug. 'Come through and tell me about it.'

'Shall we sit over by the window? I love the way the sun filters in on that spot,' Cookie purrs, moving to where we have placed the hotel's two blue-and-white-striped rattan chairs, which I am still acutely aware match neither the brown carpet nor the suite but at least help to make the room look less bare. They are placed in the far corner by the window to maximise the sunny spot and play down their presence. They also detract the eye from the awful teak units that seem to haunt that end of the room.

'So,' I sigh when we are both sitting down, 'where will you go?' I am desperately trying to beat down the disappointment welling inside me.

'Brunei.' Cookie sits back and closes her eyes, savouring the sun's rays playing on her face. I watch her and wonder what life will be like when she has gone. We enjoy an easy friendship, which, I only just realise, I have come to depend upon. I admire her for having the courage to be herself.

Cookie opens her eyes suddenly. 'You can come and visit us – it's not far away.'

The sun's heat lasering through the window suddenly seems oppressive as I study the muddy contents of the coffee mug in my hands, feeling more miserable by the minute. 'So, when do you go?'

'At the end of the month.'

'Oh.'

'Ugh.' Cookie bangs the coffee cup down on the table and throws up her hands. 'You know, that's the only thing I hate about this kind of life. You make friends and then either you leave, or they do, and you have to start all over again.' She leans over and deposits a friendly pat on the back of my hand. 'You'll be OK.'

The alternative swimming venue for me is the only hotel in town with a pool, which we check out for comparison. There isn't any, really. The manager's wife, a *farang*, is away for some reason and no one has thought to clean the pool for days. I eye it wistfully and try to will Cookie and Joe to stay. There's no way I am going to the pool at the compound on my own; I simply don't feel comfortable in that place. It isn't only the people; there's something about it, and I can't quite figure out what it is.

Monique is clearly ecstatic when Cookie and I meet her later going down in the lift. 'We move tomorrow,' she tells us from between the bodies of two Thai men shuffling in beside us. 'I can't wait, it will be so much better.' She beams at us.

'Mm, until the novelty wears off,' Cookie mutters when we reach the ground floor and Monique waves a cheery goodbye. 'That girl needs more than a change of house,' she says ominously.

This means that, apart from Harry and Grace, Mo and I will be the only expats left staying permanently in the hotel. Grace has been away for a while. I hope she will be back soon.

I have now developed a procedure for preparing the vegetables and meat. By the time I am finished, I think longingly of the supermarket vegetables back home that can be plucked off the shelf and rinsed quickly under the tap instead of the marathon session I must go through each time I came back laden from the market.

The small red book on tropical diseases helpfully recommends that all lettuce be plunged in boiling water as the only sure way to render it safe to eat. I stop short of that and treat the vegetables like dishes, running them under the tap first to get the muck off, then washing them in detergent, then rinsing off the detergent and trying not to wince when the lettuce leaves squeak every time I pick them up.

Now Cookie and Mimi have introduced me to some purple crystals, which are put into the water in minuscule amounts to turn it a pinkish colour. 'This will kill all germs,' Cookie assures me, and gives me a small jar of the stuff to start me off. I also discover that I should have been treating the chicken and pork in the same way. By the time I try to keep meat and vegetables separate, not forgetting to wash everything carefully after handling it in case of cross-contamination, I am exhausted and a serious candidate for anorexia. There is also the fact that the water from the tap is not safe to drink so everything must be given an extra rinse in bottled water.

There seem to be small crawling insects everywhere, not to mention the house lizards. Mo calls them chit-chats because of the chattering noise they make, but I rename them shit-shats after I discover that they leave little currant-like droppings tagged with a white blob all over the place.

This morning is particularly bad. When I go into the kitchen, I find droppings all round the chopping board. 'The little buggers have been having a party,' I tell Mo at breakfast. Now, as I gather up the first pile of vegetables, it takes several seconds to register that the shit-shat that I think I have just seen scurrying under the fridge has developed a weight problem and grown a fur coat.

I poke my head round the kitchen door to find Kik squatting at the door of the 'bees' balcony', as we now call it, holding the mop at arm's length, fully extended to give the tiles their daily cursory swipe. Nothing on this earth will entice her to share that space with the bees.

'We have a mouse,' I say, scrambling around in my brain for the correct words in Thai. She turns round, her face displaying an equal struggle to comprehend what is being said.

'Mouse,' I say. 'You come, see?' I pluck at words, cursing all the carefully learned phrases which never seem to apply to real-life situations. 'Em.' I grab the phrasebook and quickly flick through it. 'Under fridge.' I point to the damming spot when Kik appears at the door. As if on cue, the mouse obliges by making a suicidal dash across the floor.

'Oh!' Kik looks stunned. 'I go speak,' she says, and mutters something incomprehensible.

'I don't want to kill!' Panicking now, I give up on my Thai and jabber out in English. 'No mousetrap,' I say, miming a deathblow.

'No kill, just take away,' I say, hoping this does not translate as fast food.

'No, madame, OK, no kill,' she says, not very reassuringly.

Later she appears with a small cage. It is a humane mousetrap, I am relieved to see, and that evening we put some cheese in the appropriate place and set the trap.

Next morning, I go through to the kitchen; the cheese has gone, trap door is closed and the cage is empty. We appear to have either a thinking mouse or a very lucky one. This happens every night for a week and the mouse is now christened Houdini and seems destined to join the bees as part of the family. Houdini is also partial to bananas, and if it weren't for the fact that he makes such a mess we might have come to some arrangement.

Sunday afternoon we are sitting reading quietly when I spot Houdini scurrying along the skirting board and disappearing behind the teak units. 'Quick. Quick. Get the trap,' I stage-whisper to Mo, and point to where the mouse has disappeared. He collects the trap and we set it down at one end of the units and go to the other end to try to get Houdini to run into the cage.

After several false alarms, we finally catch him and Mo holds up the cage. 'Got you this time, you little bugger,' he says, not unkindly, as Houdini runs around the walls of the cage intent on escape. Meanwhile, I am on the telephone to housekeeping. A young man's voice comes on and I say in my best-remembered Thai that we have trapped the mouse in the cage and can they please come and do something about it.

'Got you this time, haven't we?' Mo is saying behind me, holding the cage aloft. 'You can't get out this time. Just try and get away,' which is precisely what the mouse is in the process of doing, and when I look round, it is in mid-air on its way to the floor and scurries off before we have time to blink.

'Oh, Mo! What the hell did you do? It's taken a whole week to catch the bloody thing and you let it go!'

'I didn't let it go. I didn't do anything,' Mo protests, still in a state of shock.

'Well, how did it get away then? Why the hell did you have to jiggle the cage around!'

'I didn't, it just jumped out.'

'You must have done something.'

Then I remember the guy on the other end of the phone. 'Never mind, I'm sorry, my husband has let it out. We have to try to catch it again,' I scrape up the words to say in Thai.

'I don't believe this!'

'Believe me, it just jumped out,' Mo says.

Finally, I calm down and we begin to inspect the cage. I find a loose wire, not obvious until you push at it, which was exactly what Houdini had been about to do as he scrambled around the cage looking for the precise spot. Clever little bugger. Next day a new cage is found, and the following morning Houdini discovers that breakfast comes with room included.

We go to the pub to celebrate and meet Steve, an English teacher whom we have been introduced to before and discovered only comes in on payday to get pie-eyed and legless or, as Mo would put it, rat-arsed. By the time we left the pub the first time we met him, his eyes were swimming around in their sockets.

'G'day, I'm Steve.' He's still sober at this point but can't remember us from last time, so we go through all the introductions again. I tell him the story about the mouse, including my speech in Thai over the telephone.

He sits back on his stool and looks at me, grinning. 'You know what you said to that guy,' he says.

Sensing a faux pas, I warily translate it into English.

'No. You told him you'd caught your breast in the cage.'

'What! How?' I'm horrified.

'You've mixed up the word for mouse with the word for breast,' he corrects me. He and Mo think this is hilarious. I am mortified. Ordering Thai food is a strange affair, fraught with potential mistakes, mistranslations and misunderstandings that occur somewhere between the table and the kitchen.

The first time we ever venture out on our own in the car we get hopelessly lost, as all the road signs are in Thai, apart from one that says 'steep hill'. The only other sign in English is 'rabbit' on a rabbit hutch at the place where we stop to have lunch. The menu is in Thai, no one speaks English, somehow the phrasebook has been left behind and the only thing we can remember is *cowpat*, which is the word for fried rice. They understand the *cowpat* but for some reason a complication arises until we realise that they want to know what kind of *cowpat*. We wave our hands about and shrug our shoulders. The result, we are told, is *cowpat moo*, which we think is hilarious. It turns out to be fried rice with pork and becomes our staple diet when eating out without a phrasebook.

Cookie's husband Joe is back in town again and we arrange to go out for a meal. The four of us go to a small restaurant near the hotel and order our meal Thai-style, i.e. several dishes to be shared, including fried rice. We aren't quite sure if the girl understands the order and when she comes back with water, we remind her about the fried rice. The meal arrives in stages. We really want the rice to eat along with the other dishes, so each time we ask if we can have the fried rice. When all the dishes are on the table we ask again about the fried rice. Nothing comes and we have almost finished the meal and, feeling quite full, decide to give up on the rice. A short while later, as we are thinking of leaving, three waitresses parade in smiling and bearing aloft five plates of fried rice.

The one place we do not have any trouble ordering food is at the prawn farm where we all go for lunch on the Sunday before Cookie and Joe leave. As we walk into the open-air restaurant, jumbo-size prawns are being barbecued. Even if we didn't know the word in Thai there's no mistaking what we want to order. Thank God.

Cookie and Joe have decided to invite their friends for a farewell meal. It is to be held at a Chinese restaurant in one of the hotels in town and Joe has chosen the menu and booked it for 7pm on the night before they are due to leave.

That day Cookie wants me to go with her to visit a nearby *Wat* to say goodbye to the female monks whom she has befriended. I go to her apartment, and she throws up her hands in horror. 'You will never guess what has happened,' she says. 'The hotel phoned Joe at seven this morning to ask where everyone was. They said that the meal was ready and asked when the guests were going to arrive!'

Great confusion is caused by the Thai method of telling the time. It divides the day into four sections of six hours. So 7am becomes one o'clock, 8am as two o'clock, up until midday. The process is repeated for the hours after midday and then again after 6pm, when 7pm becomes one o'clock, 8pm two o'clock, up until midnight and so on. They have different names for each time unit, i.e. early morning, late morning, afternoon, early evening and then the hours until midnight. However, Thai people do not always include these names when telling the time. You might think that you have arranged a dental appointment for 10am but the receptionist actually means 4pm. Common sense does not prevail; either that or the Chinese have some peculiar eating habits.

In the end all turns out well. Cookie is persuaded to wear a dress for once. The meal is rebooked for the evening, and everyone enjoys what turns out to be a mini version of a Chinese banquet. Someone gives Cookie a vase of red roses as a leaving present. I wish they weren't going.

Cookie and Joe come up to our apartment afterwards for a farewell drink. I inherit the roses and a small wooden house, a gift from the nuns, neither of which will fit into Cookie's already-stuffed suitcases.

The next evening, we go to the pub. It's fairly crowded with some strange but extremely fit-looking men. 'Special forces,' Guy informs us. 'You can talk to them, but they don't tell you anything about themselves or what they are doing here,' he says almost proudly. I can't help thinking he feels quite honoured that they've chosen to drink in his pub. Add that to the KGB and CIA. Maybe there's more to this place than we all know.

CHAPTER EIGHT

I miss Cookie, but thankfully Grace is back so I have someone to talk to again. Her niece Beth, who is recovering from a car accident, is taking some classes at the local university to give her something to do. This means that Grace is on her own most of the day from Monday until Friday.

Grace doesn't take kindly to the heat so must be inside most of the time, which is restricting in a place like Pits. It also means that she can be lonely on her own during the day. However, she does have quite a few Thai friends who come to visit her to practise their English and keep her in touch with what is going on.

When I arrive Chomesri, a teacher from the local school, is visiting. I tell them that I had a walk round town the day before. Halfway through, Chomesri completes my journey for me. Somehow word has got back about my movements. News travels fast. A clandestine affair is out of the question, or so I think.

I am not the only person being ignored; it seems. Mo had a call from Jacques to say that Nigel (Frances's husband) wanted to have a meeting with him at lunchtime in the canteen. According to Mo, for a whole hour Jacques did all the talking and Nigel didn't say a word, not even to say hello.

It's Mo's job to make sure that everything is done according to the oil company rules. His attitude has always been that no matter what happens during the day you don't carry it with you outside work. He is well used to having to socialise with the same people he works with. These oil people see it differently, hence the rudeness at times.

It would also appear that they are all vying with each other. They don't seem to like one another either, but tribal loyalties take over when it comes to strangers. Like wolves in a pack, they are waiting eagerly to see Mo make a mistake and fall flat on his face, as he puts it.

The evening of the party for Guy's retiral has arrived. It is being given by the oil company and it is held in the hotel owned by a Thai family and managed jointly by one of the sons and his wife, a *farang* lady.

When we arrive, everyone is gathered at the poolside where food is laid out buffet-style. We meet several new people, or at least new to me, and I am introduced to the chief engineer of the oil company, who seems a nice man. Everyone is in a cheerful mood for a change; it's amazing what a difference a free meal and drinks can make. I am desperate to see Theo's girlfriend at long last, and when we are introduced, I must admit she is a beautiful girl.

The place is decked out and decorated for the occasion, and a wheelchair is provided for the man in question as a joke. There is traditional Thai music and dancing, with several ladies who seem to be professional dancers and singers beautifully made up in traditional costumes.

Some of the Thai office staff suddenly appear, including Nok and Ying, dressed up in makeshift traditional costumes. A rather bashful Aroon has also been roped in and dressed up. They begin to dance around the room singing and eventually pick a partner from the audience. Nok persuades Mo on to the floor to dance with her. It's traditional Thai dancing with much graceful moving of the hands.

Mo hasn't a clue what he's doing but just copies Nok and makes quite a passable effort considering he hasn't had the benefit of any rehearsals. This, I now realise, is the reason for all the giggling and whispering that's been going on in the office over the past two weeks with cryptic messages delivered to Aroon to be at a certain place at a certain time and not to forget.

Several people pay tribute to Guy and sing songs; one young Thai man nicknamed Elvis (same hairstyle) is particularly good. The *farang* lady, whom we are told is called Gina, also sings a song for him; it seems that they are very good friends.

At nine o'clock the party finishes, and the talk is of everyone going back to the pub to see the evening out. 'See you at the pub then, Theo,' I call out as we are passing him on the way out.

'I'll just have to go home first to drop the girlfriend off,' he says.

'What! Why don't you bring her with you? I haven't had a chance to chat to her. Bring her with you, she'll enjoy it.'

'She's already had two Cokes and a Fanta – that's quite enough for one evening,' he says. I try pleading with him, but it's no good, so we leave him to it.

Two weeks later we are due our R&R, and since Mo must fly to Bangkok for work on the Thursday we stay on until the Sunday. We enjoy the oil company discount in the hotels they use, so we stay in the Imperial and have dinner with M at the only Burmese restaurant in Bangkok. He is friendly with the owner and the food is delicious. At the end of the meal, M's friend lays a plate on the table with long, thick, green cheroots and a dish of palm sugar. Mo, who gave up smoking years ago, eats the sugar, which I decline in favour of one of these cheroots. According to M, they are Burmese, and I just can't resist. I am in the process of giving up smoking but can still be tempted by the unusual.

Later M takes us to a hotel where we have a drink and listen to various singers, all of whom are amazingly talented. One man does an excellent impression of Elvis Presley (a popular figure in these parts) and is even better than the young man who sang at Guy's retiral.

The hotel has a large swimming pool, which I make full use of when I am not busy shopping. I buy a juicer to juice the Thai oranges, which are similar to Mandarin oranges but a fraction of the price. I also manage to find a pair of shoes my size, something that is impossible to find in Pits, and a bikini, as we have discovered that if we have lunch at Gina's hotel, we can use the swimming pool. I try the bikini on in a tiny cubicle in one of the department stores. As I turn a critical eye to the mirror, thinking the style of this bikini does a lot more for me than the one I bought in a sale at home, I find there are several heads poked round the curtain to give a friendly appraisal.

Mo is working, so I go back to the hotel to drop off my purchases and have some lunch. As I walk past the dining room, Eva is sitting at a table having her lunch. I say hello and to my surprise she invites me to join her. I sit down tentatively, but after a while I realise that this is a very different person from the woman I met before; she is really friendly. She tells me about a small shop at the airport that sells some different vegetables from the ones found in the market. Although she laughs as we chat, I still get the impression that she isn't exactly happy.

'The others think I'm mad to do my own cleaning,' she says, 'but I don't have anything else to do, so why should I get someone else to do something I do better myself anyway?' I do my best to commiserate and decide that it's probably boredom that causes these women to be so wrapped up in themselves, or perhaps everyone has simply been here too long. I feel a sudden panic and fervently hope this doesn't happen to me.

Back in Pits again, we continue the Thai lessons. Mo is so busy and so tired when he comes in from work, he doesn't have much energy left to start learning Thai, but he perseveres and continues to keep Ratana amused as her bump grows steadily bigger and bigger.

Three nights in a row we are in the pub, so on the Saturday we decide to try one of the riverboat restaurants. The menu is in Thai and English with some interesting translations. We give the girl our order and sit back to chat and wait. When the food arrives, it isn't what we ordered at all, so we tell the girl politely that there has been a mistake. 'Sorry,' she apologises, and says she got it wrong then takes it away with a repeat of our original order.

The next lot of food she brings is again not what we ordered and doesn't look like something we care to try. She looks pained, takes it away and then comes back. When I ask what happened she informs us that the cook got it wrong. We repeat our order slowly this time, ask the waitress to write it down and hope that no one else is involved in the production line. Thankfully the third time it's right. This is hard work!

Sunday is a barbecue at the pub. It's at lunchtime, so when we arrive, we join the others sitting at one of the tables outside. My only worry is that all week they have been talking about a poor pig that is to be barbecued as the main attraction. Frances and her husband are there, and Tom and Eva appear a bit later, then Theo, Max and the others. We sit around chatting; they seem to be quite friendly for a change.

After a while, the heat is too much so we go inside to eat. Mo is busy talking to Theo, Eva and Frances are sitting together, and I decide to sit down beside Tom and Nigel simply to be sociable. I try to make conversation, but they aren't exactly the most talkative pair in the world. This fits in with the revelation in the book, as I remember it, that oil company men only know how to talk to each other.

The poor pig is finally declared well and truly cooked, and we all get up to help ourselves from the spread laid out on a long table behind the island seats in the middle of the floor. When I get back to the bar with my plate, I realise that Tom and Nigel have moved away from everyone and are sitting together at the island.

I go and sit beside Mo, Theo and Max, whose company I prefer anyway, and wonder at this strange bunch of people. Monique and Jacques arrive later and sit by themselves on the other side of the bar. There's a definite atmosphere in the pub when the oil people are around. It's as if they bring it in with them.

Later, after they have gone, the whole mood of the place seems much lighter, and we all joke and have a laugh together. It's the same, I have noticed, when we first go into the bar in the early evening: we sit and chat easily with Theo and the other sundowners and Max when he comes in. The atmosphere is warm and friendly. But if the oil company people arrive it all changes and becomes almost uneasy. There seems to be some caste system whereby they avoid sitting all together, the conversation is suddenly stilted and more awkward, although Eva and Frances appear to get on well together. I wonder how these people unwind. It's as if they are constantly on show.

The good news is that our stuff has arrived from the UK. It still must clear customs, but all being well, it will arrive in Pits soon. We are looking forward to having a radio again, since everything on TV is in Thai.

The only newspaper we can get hold of is the *Telegraph*, which does the rounds of all the oil company expats before it comes to us, so the news is about six weeks old. Other than that, we have to rely on the *Bangkok Post*. This tome is the source of much amusement and seems to be the forum for complaining expats. Apparently pilfering in the postal system is rife; not even registered mail is safe according to some irate readers voicing their grievances.

News items describe thieves as having been 'nabbed' by the police, the police 'acting on a tip-off' always seem to 'expect to make an early arrest' and every accident seems to finish with 'and the truck driver fled the scene'. I have this mental image of thousands of truck drivers fleeing around the countryside all over Thailand.

It seems an unwritten law that the bigger vehicle always pays, which would explain the plight of these poor truck drivers, but for expats, they are deemed to have more money and so should at least share the cost. So, if an expat car is parked on the road and another vehicle crashes into it, the owner of the parked car is expected to pay half the cost. If you go to help someone who is hurt at an accident you can end up being sent the bill for his or her medical expenses even though you had nothing to do with causing the accident. Driving is a perilous occupation in Thailand.

It is my birthday and I have been in bed for a week with a virus, which seems to have reached its peak. I am in agony every time I try to swallow, so in the end I get up, get dressed and go down to the pub. I need some distraction to make me forget about my throat.

As is turns out it is just as well because somehow word has got out and not only am I presented with a bunch of flowers but there is also a cake. This was a complete surprise and helped to make up for the fact that I haven't yet received any birthday cards from home. It is also a welcome change for Mo, who has been living on room service all week.

Poor Mo has some work to do down near Pattaya and had arranged it so that we would go down for my birthday. In the end he manages to postpone the visit until the day after my birthday. It is a case of stay on my own here in the hotel and feel miserable or move to another hotel and at least have Mo's company in the evening. So, I drag myself out of bed on the Sunday morning and go with him.

Most of the time I spend lying by the swimming pool at the hotel in Pattaya; I don't even have the energy to swim. Anxious to cheer me up and make it a special occasion, Mo arranges for us to have a special meal to celebrate my birthday. However, I feel so bad before we get to the main course I have to go back upstairs to bed. This does not go down well.

He goes for a walk on his own later and comes back talking about all the girlie bars along the road. The next night, and in the interests of research, I decide I can manage to make the effort to go with him. It's dark and as usual we must try to avoid tripping over anything. Every bar, it seems, has several girls sitting waiting to entertain clients. Much to my surprise, when they see us walking by, they smile and wave at us to go in. I hadn't expected them to be so friendly towards another woman.

I'm not feeling much better by the time we return to Bangkok, where we meet M for a drink and a meal. Get back to Pits looking tanned and healthy but feeling awful. Still, it was worth it.

We arrive back for the weekend of the longboat race, which takes place on the river on both the Saturday and Sunday. It's a popular event, judging by the crowds who arrive to watch. Apparently, in the old days, during the Buddhist Lent period, villagers from neighbouring districts formed a boat procession to bring saffron robes to the *Wat* to clothe the Buddha image and make merit. Because there were so many longboats and people from different districts, they started racing. Since then, it has moved from being a competition between districts to competing provinces.

The stepped riverbank is packed with people, some holding umbrellas as protection from the searing sun and all cheering on their favourites to win. We haven't a clue which provinces the boats are from, but we enjoy it anyway. It also appears to be a chance for the houseboat people to get some extra cash by displaying advertising banners for the ubiquitous Pepsi and some yellow sign in Thai we can't make out. In the evening we have a meal at one of the restaurants on the river and then a relaxing lunch at a riverside bar the next day.

More Thai lessons and then Guy's birthday at the end of the week. We are all invited to help celebrate it at the pub where Mimi lays on a beautiful spread of food. It's all go.

The next night we go to another of the riverboat restaurants that we haven't tried yet. The furnishings are basic, and the forks bend without the help of Uri Geller, but this is something we have come to expect; the important thing is that the food is good. I sit back and sigh with pleasure. It's relaxing to be down on the water away from the noise of the traffic and I find something romantic about being on the river in the dark and eating by candlelight.

A large, shabby, white boat taking tourists up and down the river goes past as we are enjoying our food. Our corner table is at the water's edge on the riverside. The boat berths in front of where we are sitting, a little distance away but still close. I notice a man with his back to us is having a pee at the back of the boat. A breeze has got up and I'm aware of a fine spray, which I tell Mo I sincerely hope is either rain or coming from the ship's propeller.

Guy has a new car for his birthday and a special ceremony is held at the pub. A monk comes to bless the car and creates an intricate design on the bonnet using some kind of powder. I meet Eva as we are going into the pub. She tells me that she and Tom have suddenly been told they are leaving for another posting in a few weeks. She seems a bit shocked and although she says she is, I'm not sure if she is entirely happy, but I wish her well anyway.

Shortly before they are due to leave, she phones me. 'I heard you saying that you couldn't find scales to buy. I have some that I don't want now and wonder if you would like them. There are also some storage jars and a few other bits and pieces if you tell me what you would like.'

'Great, I'd love the scales and the storage jars, and if there is anything else that I don't need I'm happy to take them and pass them on to someone else who might need them.'

'If you would like them, I'll bring them round; otherwise I'll take them with me and give them to a charity shop,' she says, which I find a bit strange, but I'm happy to have the offer of the scales.

It's only later when she brings these things round that I realise she is extremely angry with various people. Recognising this as something she must get off her chest, I listen but don't absorb. Everyone needs to have someone to let off steam to without the details being repeated and without having to feel any regret for anything they have said afterwards, especially in a situation like this. She is teaching me a valuable lesson in expat living. I'm going to miss her.

I go to visit Grace one day and find her and Beth helping Gina to pack some stuff into boxes. 'Come in and have a coffee,' Grace says. 'We're nearly finished.' The box is taped as I sit down, and Grace goes to get some coffee. Gina and Beth go across to the table and sit chatting to each other quietly, which I think is a bit strange. I'm not having any more of this, so I start talking to them and it finally transpires that Gina is wary of me because she thinks I'm one of the oil company wives whom she has come to loathe. What a place! However, when she relates some of the stories about them I can quite see why. She is especially annoyed at the oil company attitude towards the 'contractors', as they are called, many of whom have stayed in her hotel.

A few days later I find out that Gina has left, which was what all the packing was for, and no one knows when she will be back.

The one thing I didn't think about when we came here was Christmas cards. I have a lot to send abroad, and this is predominantly a Buddhist country. We are nearing the final date for overseas mail, and I am beginning to panic. However, Grace and Beth tell me they have seen some cards in a shop downtown, so I walk down to have a look. They turn out to be OK and very light so ideal for posting abroad.

I now begin a marathon session, writing letters to everyone on the cards themselves. When I have finished a few days later I have quite a pile; I don't seal them in the hope that this will mean the postage will be less.

A fact sheet provided by the local tourist board refers to the post office as 'the office with facilities for the public', which makes it sound rather like a place you can go if you are desperate for a pee.

I normally walk from the hotel, as it isn't too far, but this does mean passing an extremely smelly drain. I have now perfected the technique of taking a deep breath and holding it until I am far enough away not to be overcome by the fumes. This is not the only drain in Pits and the worst possible scenario is to find yourself standing next to one of these noxious gas outlets when you are trying to cross the road.

The post office workers are a moody bunch, especially if you put Sellotape on anything; they push the offending item back and tell you to take it off, probably because it's a deterrent to all the pilfering that goes on. For some reason forms not written in Thai are written in French.

I anticipate having problems, so I ask Aroon to come with me. I approach the counter and ask in half Thai, half English, if I send the cards without sealing them will it be cheaper. The man looks serious for a minute, picks up one of the envelopes, examines it carefully, whilst I wait with bated breath, and then announces it will be OK. I buy the requisite number of stamps and am handed an airmail stamp. The next ten minutes is spent at a side counter with a bemused Aroon roped in to help wet and stick stamps and brand them as airmail.

CHAPTER NINE

On the outskirts of Pits is a golf course. It only has nine holes and belongs to the army, but civilians are permitted to use it, much to Mo's delight. I have promised him that if we ever know that we are going to be in one place for more than two years I shall take golf lessons.

Mo takes me at my word and introduces me to the local professional Khun Charong. For the sum of two thousand baht I can have as many lessons as necessary to get me on the course. The first lesson is booked for the next day at 4pm. Mo is still working but back in the office, so Aroon arrives to take me to the golf course.

It's a beautiful day and the temperature is cooling down a bit as I duly present myself to Khun Charong. He is a well-fed-looking man who gives the impression that he has a low opinion of females as potential golfers and unfortunately his English is limited, but what's new?

In solemn mode he hands me a golf club and we begin with exercises, twisting from side to side. After a while we progress to the more serious stuff, and I am shown how to hold the club and the rudiments of swinging and trying to hit an imaginary ball. I have a mildly successful lesson, I think, and go back home fairly pleased with myself.

My next lesson is at 8.30 the next morning. Aroon isn't needed for the first two hours, so he is taking me there and back. Again, it's a beautiful sunny day with just a trickle of cloud in the distance streaming across an otherwise clear blue sky.

This time we go straight to the driving range. As driving ranges go, this is basic. No frills, not even artificial grass, merely an area to hit balls out into the green beyond. Behind this is a large shelter for the caddies to sit and for the would-be golfers to take refuge from the beating sun or rain and perhaps quench their thirst with a drink from the ubiquitous Fanta/Pepsi machine.

A few soldiers are hanging around, much to my chagrin, as I am obviously to be their entertainment for the coming hour. Still, I do my best to ignore them and pay attention to the job in hand, namely trying to hit the ball. If Seve Ballesteros can play surrounded by crowds of people, surely, I can manage a few bored soldiers.

A bucket full of balls is duly dumped on the ground. Charong shows me once again how to hold the club and I am urged to practise my swing again and again. I am acutely aware that I'm being watched and deliberately botch my swing several times, hoping that the soldiers will get bored and go away, but eventually a ball is placed before me and I am directed to hit it.

By this time, I am terrified that I shall miss the ball and make a complete fool of myself in front of all these soldiers who are now squatting with eyes riveted to the spot where the ball lies. Like it or not, I am the main attraction, and they have the front-row seats. Nothing short of an air raid is going to move these bastards until my hour is up. Oh well.

'Madame, swing,' Charong commands curtly, and then waits, picking his nose to pass the time. I take a few deep breaths and then launch into the dreaded swing. It misses, someone sniggers and I want to commit murder, but instead I muster my dignity, pull another ball from the few sitting in front of me and try again. This time I make contact and I am so pleased I have to stop myself grabbing hold of

Charong and kissing him. Now I've got it – well, nearly. Each time I hit the ball I bring another one forward and place it ready to swing.

After several minutes, Charong has a word with one of the soldiers, who then walks across and squats down in front of the tee spot. I am now horrified to discover that he is to remain there to set a new ball for my next hit.

This completely disarms me. I cannot hit the ball properly, especially when the soldier flinches each time I go to take a swing. I try to tell Khun Charong this, but he only dismisses it with a flick of his hand and tells me to carry on. I am terrified for the man's head and my hardly acquired swing is suffering as a result. The rest of the soldiers in the meantime are avidly watching, no doubt to find out which swing is liable to separate their comrade's head from his shoulders.

When the hour is up no one is more relieved than I am. I discover that I must give the soldier forty baht, the equivalent of one pound sterling. They say life is cheap in these parts. It certainly is.

The next time I decide to state quite categorically that I do not want someone replenishing the ball and say so. Charong ignores this or simply doesn't understand, and the soldier is duly told to sit down. Once again, my swing suffers and, in the end, I refuse to do any more until the man is removed.

This is when I realise that Charong seems to think I don't want to pay the man because Aroon is now told to take the place of the soldier. A white-faced Aroon sits himself down without protest and, despite mine, gingerly places the ball at arm's length on the tee and then jerks back quickly. I give up and swing badly because I am even more acutely aware of not wanting to hurt Aroon. This continues for several more balls, Aroon looking extremely unhappy and flinching visibly. In the end, and after much gesticulating and miming of heads being chopped off, Charong finally relents and a relieved Aroon resumes the preferred position of spectator instead.

We reach a more familiar stage in our relationship, Charong and I. Now, when I hit a good ball, he positively beams, shouts out,

'Good shot, madame,' and either claps or walks across and shakes my hand. This is guaranteed to make me apprehensive because my next ball is usually terrible and he ends up with his face in his hands saying, '*Oh*, madame, why? I no see. I no see.' Then, he marches across, starts pulling and twisting my body around, saying, 'No. No cock, madame. See?' He holds my elbow out. 'This cock. This,' – my arm – 'no cock.' Which sounds rude. Biting my lips together hard against threatening hysterics, I try to tell him that it would be better to say bend, but it makes no difference.

When I make the mistake of bending my knees on the swing through, he takes the club and, in an exaggerated imitation, swings it and makes a curtsying motion, saying in a mock female voice, 'Oh, madame, *sa wa dee kha, sa wa dee kha*.' (The female version of hello.) Cheeky bugger. Aroon, whose head I could now cheerfully knock off, sits and watches with a huge grin on his face.

Finally, in an effort to improve his coaching techniques, Charong shows me what to do, moves over to the side and stands just in front of me, close to where the soldier and Aroon had to take their chances. He diligently wipes out the top of both nostrils with his thumb and tells me to swing. I ask him to move, but I am dismissed with a flick of the hand. I try again but am ignored, so I take a swing, hit the ball, which then somehow does a right turn up the front of Charong's body and hits him on the nose. I am simultaneously consumed with guilt and the giggles and have to bite my lips hard not to collapse in a heap.

He throws me a withering look but, unperturbed, demonstrates the swing again and assumes his previous position. I try to protest but am dismissed with another flick of the hand. This time I position myself carefully and take a good swing at the ball, which follows exactly the same course as before but stops short at his testicles. Thankfully, he hastily decides to move. By this time, I am bent over, knees crossed, trying desperately not to wet myself.

Mo now has a new golfing partner, Grace's husband Harry, who is away working during the week and comes back every Friday night. Harry, Beth and David, Cathy's son, another Canadian woman who is married to a lovely Thai man called Thanom, all play together at the weekend. Despite being a teenager, David is a hotshot golfer and Harry insists that Mo and I join them for a Saturday game of golf, although at the moment I only walk round.

This becomes a regular thing, as does the meal in the golf club with Cathy, Thanom, David, his younger brother, James, Grace, Harry, Beth, Mo and me. The surroundings are basic, but the food is freshly cooked and the best in Pits. It's also cheap, much cheaper than the beers to go with it.

We look forward to this one night every week that lets us be with people who aren't involved in anything to do with the oil company. None of them ever go to the pub so the conversation is fresh and stimulating without the undercurrents that swirl beneath the talk of people who work together.

My only complaint is that the toilets here are of the squat and drop variety and always seem to be awash with water. It's a tricky manoeuvre trying to squat down clutching shorts, knickers and handbag, and avoid peeing all over your feet, especially after consuming several beers.

Bea arrives, full of enthusiasm. She will be with us for ten days and is anxious to see as much as possible.

The first day I take her to the *Wat* to see the beautiful Golden Buddha. We 'make merit', as the Thais say, by paying ten baht to buy two tiny wild birds in an equally tiny cage and set them free. For the Thai people the Buddhist religion hinges on making merit in this lifetime to have a better life the next time around. Every day wild birds, turtles, fish and eels are captured, put into cages or polythene bags, or tied up and sold to the public to set free again and so 'make merit'.

The Thai people take this very seriously. Although many of them are quite poor, they seem to spend what must amount to a small fortune trying to make merit. I feel sorry for the turtles that are tied up and fish stuck in a poly bag, but I'm beginning to think the birds have it all sussed out: they spend a few hours in the comparative safety of a cage with a free meal thrown in and the guarantee of freedom at some time during the day.

As we walk along the street by the river on the way back, several Thai people stop and run their hands along Bea's arms, exclaiming at the hairs. Thai people don't seem to be at all hairy and Bea has very dark hair, which the Thais find both amazing and amusing. Luckily for them she is understanding and simply laughs the whole thing off, which is just as well; little do they know she has a black belt in karate.

The next day Mo lends us the car and Aroon for the day to go to the ancient capital Sukhothai, where the old temples have been preserved in what is now Sukhothai Historical Park. Aroon has obviously planned the whole excursion. We are held up by rain for a couple of hours, during which the three of us have lunch, but the rest of the time we drive around the ancient ruins, admiring what is left of the temples and gazing in wonder at the gigantic statues of Buddha. It is an amazing place to visit. Bea is most impressed.

We get back to Pits about six o'clock. Aroon keeps saying to me, 'Twenty minutes, madame, twenty minutes.' I think he wants to stop at his house to tell his wife he will be late, but it turns out that he wants to show us where the Buddhas are made. We are shown around the small courtyard and see lots of Buddhas at various stages of production and then one huge effigy, which seems to emanate a kind of energy that fills the whole courtyard. We stare at it in wonder. How on earth will they move it?

Aroon then hurries us across to a small museum, which, by this time, is closed, but he speaks to a young woman who seems happy to open the door for us so that Bea can have a tour around before she goes away. It is full of all kinds of artefacts, from ancient kitchen equipment to ox carts and farm tools. It is very thoughtful of Aroon to take the trouble to make sure that Bea sees all of this.

On the Thursday I take Bea to the market. She is horrified by what they do to the frogs.

Mo has a holiday on the Monday, so we decide to take Bea up to Chiang Mai. We take her to see all the tourist sights, factories and shops, plus we find some hot springs where you can boil your own eggs. We also go to the elephant-training centre to watch the elephants being put through their paces. It's fascinating to be able to get so close to these huge creatures in a natural jungle setting without any barriers and to watch them being trained to move logs under the watchful eye of their *mahouts*. Later they bathe in the river, where they are joined by the younger elephants. One of them is still a baby.

At the night market, Bea can't believe how cheap things are and buys a fake Rolex watch and Yves Saint Laurent fake handbag, Benetton shorts and top, a hand-embroidered kimono, and quite a few cassettes. Only the fact that her suitcase is already full stops her from buying more. The tourist season is beginning in earnest now, so it is really busy, but nevertheless Bea has a ball.

When we get back to Pits, she decides she would like to go to the early morning street market to see the monks collecting their alms. The farmers start coming into town late in the evening the night before. The market starts at 5am but we go down at six and she manages to get a photograph of a monk collecting his food for the day. It's like a different place at this time in the morning because the whole street is lined with people selling their produce. This is also the time when most of the locals do their shopping.

The ten days seems to fly past and Bea has a great time. Unfortunately, our visits to the houseboat restaurants result in many mosquito bites, which are probably the only genuine souvenirs she takes away with her.

The next week Mo takes me up to the golf club pro shop, and after much discussion with Khun Charong I am now the proud owner of a set of second-hand golf clubs.

Whatever my feelings about the general lack of hygiene, the market gradually becomes a place I seek to cheer myself up if I feel low for any reason. The people there are a great tonic. They will always smile and chat – the language barrier doesn't seem to matter.

I am taken aside one day and shown photographs of a trip a few of the women have gone on. Some, of course, I know better than others, but I always make a point of spreading my purchases so that I buy a little something from different stalls. That is if I can get past the woman who sells most things at the entrance to the market. If she catches my eye I am done for, because in no time at all she is stuffing potatoes, carrots, onions – you name it – into a bag before I have a chance to say no or even decide what I want.

Thai people are curious by nature and quite forthright. They think nothing of stopping me and pointing to one of my purchases to enquire how much it costs. I always hate this because invariably they inspect my purchases, frown and then tell me that I have paid too much.

They take great delight in bargaining. One baht difference is very important. It isn't at all unusual for someone to intervene in the process and bargain for me, and then, after much discussion, I am solemnly given the go-ahead to buy, even though the price has only changed from say six baht to five baht.

Aroon always intervenes on my behalf if he thinks I am being charged too much. If something is too expensive, he will shake his head solemnly and say, '*Pheng* [expensive], madame,' then he will find out why. 'Come from Chiang Mai,' or, 'From Bangkok, madame,' he will say, and point us in another direction. There are times when I have to hold my own and overrule, whereupon he will nod his head just as solemnly and say something is 'very good, madame – number one'.

The one place there is no bargaining is at the small airport shop. Aroon now takes me there a couple of times a week to see if any new produce has come in. The lady there often has leeks and French beans, amongst other things, but charges a bit more, as these are imported. Still, it helps to vary the diet.

I decide one day to make a vegetarian cashew bake, which Mo and I both like. Aroon comes with me to the market. My phrasebook doesn't cover individual kinds of nuts and I am lip-chewing over what to say when, luckily, I spot bags of cashews on one of the stalls. Some bags have whole cashews and some half or broken ones. I am about to pick up a bag of whole nuts when I remember a warning from one of Grace's Thai friends. Whole nuts are a bit more expensive than half ones, which is understandable; however, it transpires that some vendors are gluing half nuts together with latex to make them whole again.

Aroon and the vendor watch in astonishment as I put down the bag with whole nuts and pick up a bag of half nuts. The vendor says something to Aroon, who looks at me with a puzzled expression and points to the whole nuts. 'More beautiful, madame,' he says. This time, though, I don't give in; I simply smile sweetly and say that broken nuts will do. I follow this with a display of imaginary chopping to show that I will be breaking them up anyway. Aroon smiles and nods his head and explains the situation to the vendor; no one has lost face. I'm learning.

I have also been warned about buying grapes. These are plentiful in the market and stacked on the stalls in neatly tied bunches. Closer inspection, however, will sometimes reveal that certain bunches are in fact cunningly made up of loose grapes that have been painstakingly tied together with numerous rubber bands. Nothing is wasted that might be sold. A mental image of a grape pinging off the bunch and hitting someone on the nose at the dinner table some evening has me studying each bunch carefully before I buy.

The would-be supermarket, a magnanimous title, is situated across the road from the entrance to the market I normally go to.

Although it provides for many of the *farang* needs, there seems to be a complete lack of understanding as to how some of these goods should be stored. I am delighted to see that it has a refrigerated cabinet, albeit misted with condensation. When my fingers dent the butter, I take it to be a newly arrived consignment. However, several visits later, when some of the packs of butter have come to resemble the surface of the moon, and a quick inspection of the packs as yet undented reveals a thick, bright yellow, coagulated film, I realise that the condensation hiding the contents of the cabinet every morning is a result of the electricity being turned off every evening to save money. The trick is to get to the butter the day it arrives.

The shop is small and cramped, with three narrow, stomach-toning aisles, separating myriad packets and tins, balancing precariously on overstuffed shelves. To remove an item without causing an avalanche requires an IQ high enough to qualify for MENSA, but first you have to find what you are looking for. Things in here move around faster than couples on a dance floor.

The owner is a charming Chinese lady. The only cheese she buys is Edam or Gouda and the word is that if you see a new one in you buy a large piece of it and then tell everyone else, otherwise it quickly grows mouldy. You never buy the neatly cut blocks wrapped in clingfilm, especially if they have reached the sweaty stage – these are the bits she's cut the mould off. It has taken her a while to realise that no one will buy the mouldy cheese. It isn't her fault, she's trying hard, but Thai people don't eat cheese, so they don't understand how to keep it. Based on this I make an executive decision never to buy the bacon.

The one area of food I do feel reasonably comfortable with is breakfast. I daringly pluck a comforting tin of oats from the shelf, then wait with bated breath for the rest to follow. When they don't, I allow myself a little smirk of triumph.

Our usual breakfast muesli isn't available, but I have found a way of making up a version of my own, using oats and raisins from the shop and cashew nuts from the market. It is still horrendously expensive, but a better deal than buying a lot of air in a bag, which is what the cornflakes seem to amount to and cost three times the price back home. It is simply a matter of crossing fingers and hoping I get to the tins and packets before the weevils do.

There is also a department store in town that has a kind of supermarket section but caters for Asian tastes. The choice of goods is limited but OK and the salesgirls are to be found most often in front of a mirror squeezing out their spots. For some reason, a lot of Thai girls have bad skin. Computers have only just arrived here and are obviously not to be trusted because the salesgirls add everything up on the computer and then add it up again manually to check. Between this and the squeezing of spots it doesn't do to be in a hurry.

It also has a bowling alley, a restaurant and a place for having a snack lunch. But its main claim to fame for us Westerners is the coffee bar that sells real coffee made from ground beans and not the tasteless sludge that is usually served up. It's also the place to go at weekends to walk around, aimlessly enjoying the air-conditioning at someone else's expense. The only other place to go for real coffee is the nearby hotel, which has a small modern Western-style cafe for just that purpose.

At long last our things arrive from the UK. Now we can listen to the World Service on the radio, albeit straining to hear it at times as the signal fades in and out. I deeply regret not bringing more stuff, especially from the kitchen; it is so difficult to get things here and the quality tends to leave a lot to be desired; nowhere could I find a pair of kitchen scales, which is why I was so pleased when Eva offered to give me hers.

Unfortunately, it's so long since everything was packed up, I can't remember where I put the key for the trunk. Mo demonstrates a hitherto unknown knack of picking locks, and all is well. When I find the key the next night, quite by accident, my marital status is only just saved by Mo's pride in his new-found skill as a lock picker.

November is the official start of the tourist season. It's cooler at nights but still hot during the day. The hotel is swarming with 'frigging tourists and their luggage, hogging the lifts and half the bloody floor space', as Mo puts it. Like breeding rabbits, they are hastily swelling in numbers and becoming a nuisance; there's never any hot water.

It's a nightmare; the quiet sanctity of our floor, not to mention the rest of the hotel, is being invaded every night and morning with mainly French, German and Italian tourists. Their buses fill up the car park across the road – ten at the latest count – and boy do they bring a lot of luggage!

The bus tours arrive early evening, have dinner, then go on an exclusive *samlor* tour of Pits.

The trick is to try to shower before all the hot water is gone and hope that the tourists are mainly French, as for some reason there always seems to be more hot water when they are around.

We decide to go for a walk one night after dinner. It takes forever to get the lift and that's after having gone round the corner to the service one. In the end we each stand equidistant between one of the lifts and the corner, ready to pounce and hold whichever one comes first. Eventually we succeed. This becomes a nightly occurrence.

Downstairs, people are still arriving; the coffee shop is filled with tourists having dinner and even the upstairs mezzanine floor is being used. After tripping over several bags, we finally make it to the door.

Outside a warm breeze is blowing. I find it incredible that everything is just as busy in the evening as it is during the day. I still haven't got used to the fact that the shops stay open so late. Two kids scurry past, pushing me to the side. 'Why aren't these kids in bed?' I mutter, irritated by the fact that this has caused me to trip over a block of concrete, which has been set into the pavement for no apparent reason.

People and children are everywhere, and no one seems to mind not having any privacy, I've come to realise, as we pass yet another shophouse where the whole family are eating their evening meal in full view of everyone.

'That's the third lot we've seen this evening.' Mo points to the bib on the back of the *samlor* driver at the end of the snake of vehicles. The bib is stamped with the words 'exclusive tour' followed by the name of yet another of the hotels. This is to be another nightly occurrence with the arrival of the tourist season.

Each *samlor*, hood down, carries three people, two in the cab and one sitting on the back clutching a balloon as they snake their way merrily around the town, dodging the traffic.

As we make our way slowly back to the hotel along the road running parallel to the river, we hear the rhythmic banging of drums, accompanied by clanging bells and then a great cheer. 'This must be the flying vegetable show.' I perk up.

'The what?'

'I read about it somewhere. Apparently, it started with one of the cooks throwing some stir-fried vegetables to another cook who caught them on a plate. They gradually put more and more space between them until they ended up throwing them across the other side of the road. Now the tourists catch them from a platform on top of a lorry.'

As we get nearer, I say, 'They're from our hotel.' I recognise the bellboy I have declared my love to, appropriately holding the bell. He sees me and throws a cheeky grin. I'm glad it's dark. All the tables are filled with tourists, who have stopped to have a drink, no doubt relieved to have survived the traffic.

'Look.' I point to the current volunteer. He is standing on the platform, dressed in a long plastic apron and clutching an empty plate, looking eerily like a reluctant ghost that's come to dinner.

Mo and I stand side by side watching. The drum begins a steady beat, accompanied by the bells, and all eyes turn to the cook as he ceremoniously pours some oil into a huge wok surrounded by flames. Then, when it is hot enough, he throws in a pile of green leafy vegetables. There's a loud sizzling noise as he deftly stirs the vegetables. Next, he does a quick manoeuvre that sends flames shooting upwards for effect, expertly tossing and turning the vegetables several times with a few more flame-throwing tricks for good measure until finally, as the drum roll and bells get louder and more frantic, he tosses them in the direction of the hapless tourist on the platform, waiting nervously with plate in hand.

A great cheer goes up as the vegetables make it halfway onto the plate. If the person catches them, they don't have to pay, or so the story goes.

'He looks pleased with himself,' Mo says as the man holds up the plate, vegetables dripping off the side, and grins at the assembled company. I can't get rid of the vision of some poor guy ending up with a green wig. We get back to the hotel tired and looking forward to an early night away from all the clamour and noise outside, although tonight it seems even more noisy than usual.

'Must have left the TV on,' Mo says as we walk out of the lift.

'We never have it that loud, do we?' I say, but hope it isn't one of Mo's 'frigging tourists' to blame. If it is, we're in for a bad night.

We open the door. It's much worse. The noise is coming from the *Wat* across the road. They have turned the ground outside into an outdoor, seemingly all-night cinema. The fact that we can hear every word and have a bird's-eye view of the screen does nothing to help. Neither does going to bed and pulling the covers over our ears. It goes on for days, or rather, nights. The *Wat* needs some money, and this is their way of collecting it.

In the mornings now we get up, bleary-eyed from lack of sleep, shower and have breakfast, and then I go with Mo to help catch the lift. He presses the bell for the corridor lift, whilst I rush round to press the one for the service lift, then we wait in the prescribed manner. It's extremely stressful if you have to do it on your own.

Sometimes I go down to the office with him to save Aroon having to come back for me and face the mayhem again. It really is like an assault course now, bags and people are everywhere, and poor Aroon arrives, agitated because he can't get near the car park. We have got to go.

We start looking for a house. Grace is devastated and warns me again of the perils involved, but Mo is adamant, and I have to say I don't blame him; I'm fed up with cold showers in the morning.

Peter, young contractor and hunky M&B hero-type, has just left and the house he rented is now available. This also has the added attraction of having a swimming pool. We go to look.

The house is set back in a huge walled garden just off the main road on the outskirts of the town. There are two houses. A large house, which the landlord lives in with his family and a smaller house adjacent to it. A long, straight driveway leads up to both houses and then forks off to the smaller one on the right. I am wary of the basketball stand sitting in front of the house at the end of what could be our driveway.

The gardens are lovely, with rows of mango trees down either side and a small pond in the middle with a bridge draped over it, reminiscent of the willow pattern china. The swimming pool, fenced in at the back of the smaller house, is about the second best in town and big enough to have a good swim. My heart is thumping.

Sadly, the house is a disappointment. It only has two bedrooms, one downstairs with an en-suite bathroom, which also opens onto the lounge, and one upstairs. The whole top floor is split into a huge bedroom with a large dressing room, which could at a pinch be used as another bedroom, and a huge bathroom. It was originally all one bedroom, but someone had a wall built to split it up.

Downstairs, apart from the bedroom and bathroom, is a small kitchen, which has an equally small wooden table complete with wonky leg and two chairs that have seen better days. The rest is a lounge area with a sink down one side where there used to be a bar.

The landlord, Khun Choochai, is Chinese and rumoured to be extremely rich. His family owns one of the hotels in town. When I note the absence of a dining-room table, he points to the kitchen. 'But what about when we have guests?' I say, horrified.

'Then you take them to eat in the hotel,' he says, as if this were the only thing to do. When I point out that this is not good enough, he is astounded at first, then agrees we can have a dining-room table.

The biggest problem we have is the wallpaper. Not only is it not even remotely to our taste but it has been up so long it is very dirty; in fact, the paper upstairs has a hessian texture and is engrained with dirt. We agree to take it if he will paint it, we say.

He is shocked. 'But it does not need painting,' he says, incredulous at the very thought. We are adamant.

Khun Wipa, his wife, is summoned. She is even more incredulous. She pats the wallpaper. 'Very beautiful,' she purrs.

'Very dirty now,' I say. 'Better to take off and paint. No paint, we no take.'

Khun Choochai translates. She looks horrified.

There follows what appears to be the beginning of a divorce as they confer in rapid-fire speech, with Choochai obviously quickly losing ground.

'Cannot,' he says finally. 'It will take too much time to take the paper off the walls and paint it.'

Zeb, the big boss, comes to pay us a visit. Mo takes him to see the house and he makes some comment about it being more managing director level as they go up the driveway. 'Wait until you see the house,' Mo tells him. It isn't so much the house that has him agreeing to it if we want it, but the fact that the rent is about half the amount we are paying for the hotel.

'We'll only move if the electricity and water are included, and a maid service,' Mo insists. There's no way we are moving for it to cost us money and all these things are included in the rental of the hotel apartment. Amazingly he won't agree to this, so we are back at square one until M intervenes and common sense prevails. The rent is raised a bit more to include what we want. However, we still won't budge until the place is painted.

In the pub one night, Ziggy announces that he is leaving. He seems to have fallen out with his landlady and is going to Bangkok. This means that his house will be available for renting.

A couple of weeks later, we meet another *farang* couple; the husband, Sergi, is a contractor, and his wife Lea is from Singapore but speaks fluent Thai. She knows of a house for rent and offers to act as interpreter.

The house turns out to be the one Ziggy and his wife have vacated. It sits in its own grounds and is enormous for only the two of us. It's a bit more expensive than the smaller house but still much cheaper than the hotel. There's no comparison between the two houses; this one has three bedrooms inside, plus two outside and maids' quarters. This has everything we would need and more: a TV, video, stereo, telephones everywhere and an intercom system to call the maid or the gardener. The garden isn't nearly as nice and has no swimming pool, but it is near the golf course and the dreaded compound.

The landlady's husband is a colonel in the army, as far as we can gather, and the hunky-looking gardener, who also acts as a security guard, is a soldier. The landlady and her husband have a house on one side with a fence in between and some soldiers live in the house on the other side.

We sit at the table with Lea, the landlady, Mo and me. It is obvious that this woman desperately wants us to take this house, but I'm not sure. It really is too big. Besides the three bedrooms, which we would like, it has various other rooms and a large kitchen. I know I wouldn't feel comfortable living here on my own if Mo had to go away for any length of time. Much to the lady's chagrin we tell her we'll think about it.

A few days later Lea phones to ask if we are going to take the house. I tell her we're still thinking about it but I'm not keen.

A few days later, again Lea phones. 'I wish you would take it; this woman keeps phoning me asking why you don't like it; she can't believe you don't want it.' I won't be hurried.

In the meantime, we look at another house, a new one this time and very nice, but the owner wants a year's rent in advance so that she can build a wall around it.

The big event in Thailand in November is Loi Krathong, which is held on the night of the full moon. The last three weeks in October, and the first three weeks in November are the twelfth lunar month in the Thai calendar. It is the height of the rainy season, when the *klongs* (canals) are filled with rainwater. Parts of Bangkok are flooded and houses up-country are surrounded by *klong*-jars filled with water stored for drinking and cooking during the hot dry months – according to the guidebooks.

The Thai people celebrate this abundance of water by *Loi* (floating) the *krathong*, a hand-made creation which can be extremely elaborate or, more usually, a candle inside a small boat fashioned from a banana leaf. In Pits they put paper money in the boat, light the candle, float it, *wai* and make a wish. If the candle is still burning when it floats out of sight good luck is ensured for the coming year, or so we are told.

In the evening we stroll along to the river. Crowds of people are all along the stepped bank and the water is glistening with the lights from hundreds of candles as the *krathongs* silently float on the water. It's a beautiful and poignant sight. As we walk back down the river, we notice that the current is carrying many of the *krathongs* back into the side of the river where a group of kids are busy collecting the money.

It is now December and a holiday for the king's birthday, so we decide to go to Mae Sot, a small town on the Burmese border. I begin to regret it on the way; the road is so full of bends I feel sick, and I am mightily relieved when we finally arrive.

It has only one hotel and it's quite new. It is also offering special rates for this weekend, which is why we have come. Things seem quiet in the late afternoon, and we wander around outside for a while taking photographs and admiring the view over the river. The evenings are much cooler here, I find out later, and I really wish I had brought warmer clothes.

Dinner is Thai food, which we enjoy. They have no such thing as wine to drink, but I have discovered a cocktail called Mai Thai that's strength depends upon its maker. They are very moreish, but these are quite tame, so all is well.

'Whatever you do, don't ask for brown bread here; they won't have any, and I want to get out of here before lunchtime,' Mo warns the next morning. So, strongly resisting the urge to try, I have porridge instead. Later we drive around for a bit and then go up to the town itself.

Just on the outskirts and alongside the river is a large market. The vendors appear to be Burmese, and we find lots of places selling gemstones; however, you really must know something about them to know whether or not you are getting a bargain, but it's good fun to wander around looking. Despite the cool evening the day is blistering hot, which is a good excuse to while away the time in the covered stalls and shops that sell the gems as well as the others selling Burmese antiques and artefacts. I spot some Burmese cheroots and buy them. 'I'm going to give Beth a couple of packets as a Christmas present,' I tell Mo.

Farangs are not allowed to cross the border, which is a narrow river, so we must content ourselves with watching the activities as the Thais and Burmese come and go quite freely. Curfew must be at sunset because at five o'clock there seems to be a great rush to get back across to their respective countries, especially the Burmese.

It's just as well the river is narrow, as they pile so much stuff and so many people into each boat they would sink if the river had been any wider.

That evening a celebration seems to be going on; the hotel is packed with Thai people attending a function. Unfortunately, they have also brought their children, who are left in the charge of their nannies. The foyer of the hotel has an enormously high cathedral-style ceiling, which provides the perfect acoustics for little voices to let rip.

Having had dinner and then gone for a walk, we decide to have a drink in the foyer, for want of somewhere better to go. Now, as these children appear from nowhere, we sit in a state of shock whilst they run around screaming and yelling, converging on the empty bandstand to whirl around on a stool, bang on the piano, jump over the backs of the seats and generally create mayhem. It is like being in the middle of an animated Giles cartoon. The nannies have no control, and the parents are too busy enjoying themselves to notice. We are completely mesmerised by the mayhem going on around us and silently hoping they won't be occupying any of the rooms on our floor. Later we find out that unfortunately our worst fears have been realised. We wonder if Thai children ever go to bed.

The next weekend also has a holiday Monday attached to it so, as it coincides with our R&R, we fly down to Bangkok. This time we scour the shops to see what is on offer that is worth buying. We find some nice rattan furniture and discover a shop near the Oriental hotel that sells bronzeware. After much deliberation we buy a hammered bronze salad bowl and sugar and cream set that are polished bronze on the inside and matt black on the outside. We decide we'll buy some cutlery to match later.

Afterwards we can just afford a snack lunch at the Oriental, where we sit outside on the terrace overlooking Bangkok's busy Chao Phya River.

The favoured place for *farangs* to food shop in Bangkok is Villa Supermarket. Each week the oil company has boxes of groceries delivered from here to their people in Pits. We enjoy no such luxury so must make do with what we can take with us on weekends like this. We always go with the idea that we will buy some meat to supplement the chicken and pork diet, but space is limited so, getting our priorities in the right order, we end up with wine and cheese. This is also the only place I can buy large tins of olive oil for cooking and wholemeal flour for bread.

We can get some wine in Pits, but the choice is extremely limited, and we never know how long the shop has had it nor how it has been kept. When I took the first bottle I bought back to complain that it was sour, the man took it from me, obviously thinking I simply didn't like it and he was doing me a favour by getting rid of it. My second purchase, a bottle of Rioja, had to be thrown out.

Khun Choochai phones Mo to arrange for another meeting re the house. In the meantime, Lea has been phoning me to find out if we are going to take the other one; the landlady is still hassling her every day to find out what is wrong with the house and why don't the *farangs* like it?

Included in the rental of the small house is the offer that their maid will do the washing and ironing. As we wander round the property, we come across the maid doing the washing; she is sitting on the ground with two large basins, one full of soapy water, the other clear water. I watch with a horrified fascination as she takes a shirt, lays it on the ground and proceeds to scrub it vigorously with a bar of soap. I have heard that the Thais are diligent about removing stains – there might not be much material left when they have finished but the stain will be gone. *Why, I wonder, if this man has so much money, do they not have a washing machine?*

We reach a Mexican stand-off over the wallpaper. Khun Wipa will not relent, and neither will we. Life's a bitch.

The 'bloody computer' has now taken the hump and stopped working, or 'crashed' as they say. I think Mo secretly blames me for what he calls my negative attitude towards it. Anyway, it has been taken to Bangkok to be fixed, which means I get a holiday from going into the office for a while. I secretly hope it will prove to be a write-off and then it might be replaced by a recognisable brand name.

Unfortunately, my respite is short-lived. The 'bloody computer' proves to be fixable and arrives back in the office the next week. Oh well.

Thai generosity can be quite overwhelming at times. The Thai friends who go to visit Grace would never dream of turning up without taking something along – usually edible. Thai people also have a very sweet tooth; almost everything has sugar in it, including the majority of milk sold in Thailand. Even the savoury dishes normally have a teaspoon, or a tablespoon, of sugar added. As a result of this the Thai diet can do damaging things to the *farang* waistline.

Grace and Beth are both beginning to suffer and so they try to steer the conversation around to more savoury items of food. When they discover that a good friend keeps quails, hoping this will lead to better things, they let it be known that they are very fond of quail. However, on the next visit, instead of the expected birds they are presented with a whole lot of quails' eggs, which, as Grace puts it, neither of them cares to try.

To refuse would cause loss of face for the person giving the gift, so nothing is ever declined. It is also difficult to give things away because everyone seems to know everyone else and the maids are extremely nosy, so even giving something to another *farang* is a bit dodgy.

I laugh too soon when Grace is presented with a second batch of eggs, because by this time I have met her Thai friend, who is a lovely lady, and apparently, she has left a batch of eggs to be given to me.

My quandary is whether to try to hatch them out on the balcony (bearing in mind we are on the eleventh floor) or stuff them in the fridge and look for recipes. Delicacy or not, there's just something about eating such a small bird's eggs. In the end I put them in the fridge. I do try to do something with them, but boiled they still make us feel like heels for eating them, and I feel like a murderess when I crack any of them open to disguise them in an omelette. After a few attempts I give up. Unfortunately, I don't seem to have made much impression on the numbers.

Thai lessons have been suspended temporarily. Ratana is now the proud mother of a baby boy nicknamed Gop, which means frog, apparently, because that's what he reminds her of. Most Thai people have nicknames in addition to formal names. This dates back to an era of high infant-mortality rates. The formal name was registered but a nickname was used to deceive the spirits into believing that the child did not exist.

It's the oil company annual Christmas party and we are invited. When we get there, the only person who speaks to us is Theo. He introduces us to some people who have come up from Bangkok. The bigwigs are also there: chairman, wife and hangers-on. The others ignore us, which seems strange, but we have got used to it now and carry on regardless. It's a free meal if nothing else.

We end up sitting at a table with Theo and some others from Bangkok. From where I am sitting, I have a clear view of the bigwigs' table and my eyes are drawn to one of the wives who appears to have a perfectly coiffed hairdo that never moves. Her head moves but her hair stays in place; it must be solid with hairspray. The guy sitting beside me introduces himself as Bill. He's starving, he tells me; he hasn't had anything to eat since lunchtime, poor guy. 'Never mind,' I say, 'the food is sure to be good.'

There are a lot of people and by the time the food is served we are all really hungry. The first course is brought in. It's tepid shark's fin soup, and someone suggests adding some whisky to improve the flavour. Hot, I can take it, but tepid is something else; it's like eating slime. Everyone feels the same way and we wait for the next course.

This time a pot is brought in and put in the middle of the table for us all to help ourselves. 'What is it?' I ask the waiter.

'Chicken stew,' he says.

Bill is desperate and asks if anyone minds if he goes first. 'Go ahead,' I say eagerly. 'This will be good.' Bill picks up a serving spoon and fork and reaches in. We all watch in horror as the head of a chicken appears, followed by a scrawny neck and the rest of its body, including the feet, complete with claws. Bill slowly lowers it back down into the pot and we all sit there staring at it. No one makes a move except one guy's Chinese girlfriend, who decides she will have some.

'I just couldn't,' Bill says quietly.

'I know,' I say, and we sit there gazing sadly at the pot like mourners at a funeral.

The next plate is filled with slimy mushrooms, which prove to be almost impossible to get hold of. Some green, tepid vegetables appear which don't fill much of a hole and then a crispy duck. The only problem is that the meat has been removed and the crispy skin stuck back in small squares to be picked off and eaten. Even the Chinese girl baulks at this. 'I never see this before,' she says. 'What have they done with the meat?' That's what we'd all like to know. Things are getting desperate now. The next thing to come is a large plate piled with fried rice.

'Oh, thank goodness, at last this really should be OK,' I say. We all wait eagerly and then help ourselves. I was right: it is fried rice – only problem is, it's stone cold.

Just before the coffee arrives Theo decides he has an urgent phone call to make and slips off, lucky bugger. The rest of us must watch a skit put on for the bigwigs by the ladies from the compound.

The quails' eggs are still there a few weeks later at Christmas. Grace decides to buy a turkey and invite all her friends for Christmas dinner, including us. Apparently, she did something similar on her last trip out here. She provides the turkey and vegetables and gets the hotel to cook the meal. Not trusting them with the stuffing, she makes this herself.

On the appointed day all goes well until the last minute. We take some wine and go down to the dining room slightly early in case Grace needs some help. Cathy, who has made an apple pie, is also there. As we stand chatting to our anxious hostess, a waitress interrupts to say that someone in the kitchen wants to ask her about the chicken pie.

Grace turns white and, with a look of horror, dashes frantically to the kitchen. A few minutes later she comes back, her face a picture of profound relief. It transpires that for some reason they think that the stuffing, which she has cooked in a baking tin, is a chicken pie. The turkey is intact.

It seems strange to be eating Christmas dinner when the sun is shining outside, but we have a wonderful meal and afterwards all go upstairs to exchange presents. As we sit chatting, my eyes roam nonchalantly over the makeshift Christmas tree (a huge green plant tastefully adorned with tinsel) and the pile of neatly wrapped presents below.

My eyes rest on three beautiful baskets in the shape of top hats, decorated with paper streamers. Then I notice the contents. They are filled with the dreaded quails' eggs. As there are only three *farang* families in the room, including ourselves, it isn't hard to guess who they are for.

I catch Grace's eye and direct her gaze to where the baskets sit. Her jaw drops open and then snaps shut again, but her eyes hold the full horror of her thoughts as she mentally tries to stuff more quails' eggs into an already straining fridge.

CHAPTER TEN

Cookie and Joe decide to come and visit us at New Year. I make a chicken curry for them, which is just as well because what should have been a four-hour flight takes about two days due to delays. However, they finally arrive for Hogmanay on the evening flight.

The curry has been maturing nicely and keeping the three dozen quails' eggs company at the back of the fridge. With rice it provides an excellent stomach lining for the evening to come. We're off to the pub to see in the New Year. Where else?

Everyone who is anyone is there, of course, and we manage to remain reasonably sober until midnight. After that it is every man and woman for themselves. Much drinking and merriment ensues and falling about trying to dance, clinging on to partners, and in the end general good-natured mayhem ending in chaos with everyone staggering to their cars about 4am, or so I seem to remember the next day.

Cookie and Joe proclaim themselves happy in their new posting and spend what little time they have left renewing old acquaintances and visiting favourite places.

Cookie does tell me that when they arrived in Brunei, she met two of the women at the local shop, who asked which house she lived in. 'I told them two houses down from the managing director's house,' she says. 'They were not pleased.'

'Why?'

'Because I didn't tell them in which direction.'

'So?' I am puzzled.

'So, they didn't know whether they should speak to me or not. They didn't know what Joe's job title was, so they didn't know if I was on their level or not. So, after that they didn't speak to me.'

'You're kidding me.'

'No. As a matter of fact, we were only staying there temporarily and then we moved, and Joe was promoted and now the ladies speak to me quite happily because he is on the same level as their husbands.'

If this is what happens in a large community it must make for an awkward situation on the small compound they have here. No wonder we are ignored.

We go to the pub the night before they leave. It's full of people, and Cookie and I are sitting near the end of the bar. Everyone is talking and laughing, and I realise a strange man is sitting next to me who doesn't seem to know anyone and who hasn't spoken a word. Hating to see anyone left out and spurned on by a couple of glasses of *wai si kao*, I introduce Cookie and myself.

'So where are you from?' Cookie asks.

'Australia,' he answers quietly.

'And what do you do for a living?' I boldly enquire.

His mouth forms into an enigmatic smile. 'I can't really say.'

'What do you mean?'

'Well, it's a secret,' he says, the tiny smile playing on his face.

'Come on, you can tell us.'

'Yeah,' Cookie joins in.

Enigmatic smile. Silence. Then: 'I work for the Australian Government.'

'Oh? What's so secret about that? What do you do?' I persist obstinately.

Same patronising smile. 'I'm a kind of a spy,' he says smugly.

'Oh, well!' I say, leaning back. 'You've come to the right place then. Max over there is employed by the CIA. Ziggy, who was here but still visits, we think is involved in the KGB, the special forces guys come in on a regular basis, and my husband and I are thinking of applying to MI5 to represent the British contingent.' Cookie nods wildly in support.

That wipes the stupid smile off his face. This Mona Lisa in trousers obviously thought he was sitting next to two daffy females and would have a laugh at our expense.

We have just finished dinner and decided for once to have a night in. The phone rings and it's Beth. 'Have you seen the fire?'

'What fire?' I feel eleventh-floor panic creeping up my spine.

'It's down by the river. Come up and see.'

We take the lift upstairs and there are Grace and Beth looking out of the window at the far end of their corridor. 'Come and see this.'

The sky is filled with thick smoke and yellow flames. 'Looks like one of the shophouses has caught fire,' Mo says, 'and the way they are all jammed up together it's spread to all the rest of them.'

It's a spectacular sight but also tragic. At the very least people have lost their homes, and worst of all it seems to be across the road from the hospital, which, judging by the severity of the fire, will surely have to be evacuated. We just hope no one is hurt. Beth and I take photographs from the window, which, being on the top floor, affords the best view.

According to a report in the *Bangkok Post* a row of twenty-three two-storey wooden houses burned down and the damage was estimated at about five million baht. When Mo and I go to have a look a couple of days later, we see that the fire wasn't only near the police station but also that the walls of the hospital across the road are black so it must have been a close shave. It's at times like this I wish we didn't live so high up.

A few weeks later Mo has work to do in Bangkok, so we make it our R&R. He will be busy Wednesday, Thursday and Friday. The manager of the firm he is visiting invites us out for a meal. Mo agrees to go once the job is completed. On the Saturday one of their men picks us up in a car early evening and drives us to a riverside restaurant which specialises in seafood. I notice he seems indifferent to traffic lights, but we get there in one piece, so I don't dwell on it.

Mo loves seafood and, although I am not a fan, the food is quite tasty. The place is open-air with a roof overhead and lots of Thai people are eating already. We seem to be the only *farangs*. Our hosts are the guy who drove us here, the manager and his girlfriend. Their English is limited so conversation is a bit difficult at times, but we muddle through. I do notice as the evening wears on that our driver, who has been knocking back the beer with gay abandon, is becoming merrier by the minute. In fact, I'm sure he's pissed. I murmur my concern to Mo as we leave the restaurant, but he seems to think that there's nothing to worry about and points out that the guy is walking and chatting normally.

My worst fears are realised on the drive back as he proceeds to drive through every red light until he finally hits another car. It had to have seen us coming, but Thai men are so macho about this kind of thing. Our car bounces off the kerb but miraculously it doesn't turn over and no one is hurt.

Luckily, the other guy and his girlfriend have been following us and he gets out of his vehicle to take charge of the situation. We are given strict instructions to stay put in the back of the car in case the other driver realises that we are *farangs* and thinks he can capitalise on it. We watch as much discussion takes place then all three men part company and the guy in charge, who is full of apologies, and his girlfriend take us back to our hotel.

'The next time anyone invites us out like this,' I tell Mo, 'I don't care a stuff about loss of face. We arrange our own transport.' He agrees.

On the Saturday we decide to be tourists for the day and go on a river cruise from the Oriental hotel to Ayutthaya, the ancient capital of Thailand. Half the trip is made by bus either coming or going and the other half by boat. We decide to travel up by bus in the morning as we guess that the river might be misty then and we wouldn't see much.

The bus party is a mixture of *farangs* and Asians. I watch everyone as they board the bus and note that one girl is particularly striking. She is tall with model-like looks and a mass of pleated hair. My attention is also drawn to a family of Americans consisting of mother, father and two grown-up sons. To be truthful, it's the eldest son who has caught my interest. He is tall with dark hair and quite good-looking. I am back in writer's mode again.

All goes well until our first stop. We all get off the bus to look at some ancient ruin, wander around for a bit in the heat, looking suitably impressed, and then traipse back on the bus. For some unknown reason, the tall *farang* girl decides to sit in a different seat.

Well, this causes all sorts of consternation. She is also an American and informs the people who have now been split up that none of the seats are booked so she can sit wherever she likes. Luckily, they are also *farangs* so World War Three is postponed. It's amazing how one tiny, thoughtless decision like this can completely change the atmosphere, which is now heavy with resentment from several quarters. I can't help wondering why the stupid cow can't simply go back to the seat she started in, and we'll all be happy again. But no. Talk about drawing attention to yourself!

Luckily, there are no more stops. If there were, it is doubtful if anyone would be prepared to get off the bus. As the trip progresses, I notice that the American family is becoming friendly with the woman hitherto hell bent on making everyone's life a misery. The eldest son is obviously quite taken with her. I have now lost interest in the ruins and am plotting a book. The only trouble is that the heroine in this case seems to be older than the would-be hero, so perhaps I'll have to do a rehash.

Once we have 'done' the ancient city, we board the boat that will take us back down the river to Bangkok. It has an excellent buffet on board, set out on a table in the middle of the main passenger area. Mo goes up one side and helps himself to some food, and I go up the other side. I must be psychic.

Later we go up on deck to sit outside and watch the scenery as the boat cruises gently down the river. As luck would have it the Americans, including my new hero and heroine, are sitting opposite us, so I can enjoy the passing scenery and eavesdrop at the same time. She is telling a story about a friend of hers who has always worn sunglasses no matter what the weather was like or where she was going. Now that she is older, apparently she has absolutely no wrinkles around her eyes. He is hanging on her every word and so am I. I am swearing an oath to a lifetime behind shades when I realise that this isn't how it should be at all; she is supposed to worship him.

Eventually I decide he's a bit wimpish and lose interest. The river has more to offer. The houses here are on stilts and we watch some boys dive into the murky waters to splash and swim. It's at this point that the guide reminds us that the people who live on the river use it for all their basic needs, which is a bit disconcerting when we pass one man cleaning his teeth. Besides the human occupation, we see lots of birds to exclaim at as we chunter along.

The next morning, we are due to fly back up to Pits. Mo has been extremely ill during the night and looks like death. We wonder if it was the buffet and I'm glad I chose to go up the other side. For a while it looks as if he won't make it out of bed, but later in the morning he rallies and we can leave.

I am still working with the girls, helping them to learn how to use the 'bloody computer'. I have discovered that Ying, who does the filing, has a master's degree in English. But Nok, who types the letters, doesn't seem to have much of a clue. She seems to rely on Ying to correct her mistakes or simply leaves them and Mo then must redo them himself, which isn't how things are meant to be. If he could swap them round, we realise, one of his many problems would be solved. There is also the matter of when Nok goes on holiday or is sick, Mo has no one to take over.

Ying can't type, but I have brought my typing books with me (for some strange reason), and I set about encouraging her to learn to touch-type. She is a willing and able student, but much more pedantic than even I am. When Nok is away on holiday and Ying is typing the letters, she will print the thing out again and again if even a full stop is missing, which is bad news for the trees.

One afternoon, when I am in the office helping, Mo is anxious to get a letter off that same day and we have to literally yank it from her hand so that he can sign it. After three print runs, she discovers that she has missed out a comma and refuses to hand it over.

I am working on getting to the stage where I can sit at home at the other end of the telephone but doing something useful like getting on with my book, instead of sitting at Mo's desk reading the paper, ready to leap to Ying or Nok's assistance when something goes wrong. They can do the monthly printout themselves now, but they are so nervous about something going wrong, I'm afraid Ying will either wet her knickers or become permanently knock-kneed if I don't turn up.

They are lovely girls and always dress for the office as if they are going out for the evening; it's a treat to go in and see what they are wearing today. By our standards it's way over the top for daywear, but at least they take pride in their appearance.

I am now on my fourth cold and Mo has had three since we came here. Grace, Harry and Beth have also been suffering. Grace thinks it has something to do with the air-conditioning. I finally go to the chemist and ask him for a tonic because I feel terrible.

I think he has taken me literally because this stuff he has given me is foul-tasting. The list of ingredients reads more like embalming fluid. It has creosote in it, amongst other things, so I suppose if nothing else I should be well preserved. I do wonder, though, if perhaps something got lost in the translation and his English wasn't as good as I thought it was.

I must admit, it has made me feel better, but Mo reckons that's because it's eleven per cent proof.

I am at the hairdresser again for my usual Princess Di hay cut. We are getting on well, the hairdresser and I; we're now quite chatty. This time, after he finishes cutting my hair, one of the girls is commandeered to dry it and he sits himself down on a stool next to me. 'Tomorro, I go fo operation,' he tells me solemnly.

'Oh dear.' I look horrified. 'What for?' I am really concerned.

'This,' he says, whereupon he unbuttons his shirt and pulls it open to expose his left breast.

My body stiffens. I didn't think we were that chatty. I don't think I want to know.

'This,' he points to his left breast, 'this grow bigger than this,' he says, exposing his right breast. 'You see?' He points.

'Oh. Yes. Mm.' I nod my head, eyes fastened on the little mound. 'Tomorrow they cut.'

'Ugh!' I don't want to hear the rest, but I am tethered to a hairbrush pulled taut by the girl wielding the dryer and now, caught up in the drama, pulling even tighter. I can't move.

'Yeah, cut.' He mimes a slice past the offending mammary.

'Ugh.' I wince, wishing he would put it away. My arms form a protective shield around my own mammeries as I frantically try to think of something to say to change the subject. Thankfully, the phone rings.

When I get back to the hotel, I go in by the side entrance. It's that time in the afternoon when there is a lull before the tourists arrive. For a moment I think that I have walked into a time warp: the reception staff and bellboys, plus Khun Pornsak, are standing around like statues. I am puzzled for a moment until I hear voices and realise that they are all watching the afternoon soap opera. I swear I could pick up a chair and walk out without anyone noticing.

Our next long weekend we head off to Chiang Rai in the north of Thailand. We drive up on Saturday and plan to come back on Monday. The journey is every bit as seat-gripping as usual, with high-speed buses, smoke-belching lorries, police speed traps (I spy one policeman hiding up a tree) and those out to test their fate for that day or trying to make it to the afterlife in a hurry.

Chiang Rai is relatively unspoilt and, like Pits, people use it as a base to visit places of interest. The big attraction up here is the Golden Triangle, which of course is set up for tourists but is interesting to see. However, to be honest, unless someone pointed it out you wouldn't really know which part belonged to which country, they are all so close together.

It's a sensitive area by all accounts as far as *farangs* are concerned. The Thai people can come and go as they please and provide boat trips for tourists round the river so that *farangs* who like to live dangerously can risk being shot at. We play safe and buy the obligatory photo, three photos joined together, showing the infamous triangle.

We also go up to Mae Sai, a small town at the northern-most point in Thailand right on the border with Burma. Here there seems to be a thriving business selling all kinds of goods, especially shoes, to the Burmese. We are allowed to walk three quarters of the way across the bridge separating the two countries, but no further. It feels strangely uncanny to be so restricted when all the Thais and Burmese can come and go as they please.

On our way back to Chiang Rai we decide to visit a Buddhist temple, which turns out to be up a mountain. We are now in the foothills of the Himalayas. I can't believe how steep it is; it's like a prolonged take-off in an aeroplane. We climb to about 6,500 feet, so Mo helpfully informs me, and seem to drive for miles up a narrow, twisting road going higher and higher. The scenery is quite fantastic if you like that sort of thing and don't suffer from vertigo, but all I can think of is having to drive all the way back down again. When we reach the top, I am surprised at how many people are there and hope they won't all decide to go back down at the same time. We walk around, but I'm so busy worrying about the forthcoming descent, I can't concentrate on anything. When we eventually get back into the car, I close my eyes and tell Mo to let me know when we reach the bottom.

When Mo announces that we are safely back on ground level I can face the world again and let out a sigh of relief as we begin our drive back to our hotel in Chiang Rai.

After our meal, we go for a walk, forever hunting out bargains for ourselves and our shopping-mad friends. T-shirts, polo shirts, fake big-name shorts and trousers are the in thing and so incredibly cheap it begs the question, what did the people who made these get out of it?

After a while we tire of this and go for a coffee in a small cafe. I ask for two coffees and the girl taking the order keeps going on about tea. I keep on asking for coffee and she keeps on about this damn tea until a man with an American accent, who turns out to be the owner, intervenes.

'I keep asking for coffee and she keeps going on about tea,' I say, wondering how on earth she can have got it so wrong.

'Actually,' he says, 'she's just confirming your order for two coffees. In Thai *song tee* confirms that you want two things.'

'Oh.' I am suitably deflated, and our coffee arrives at last. We obviously haven't tackled the finer points yet. I apologise profusely to the girl, who smiles and says, '*Mai pen rai*' (never mind) but is probably thinking what a total prat this woman is.

The weather is beginning to change again. I think we're going into summer. Apparently it gets very hot. I can't imagine it getting much hotter during the day than it does now, but at least Pits has a better climate than Bangkok.

Mo's new hobby is collecting stamps. This is to take his mind off the frustration of working with both the oil company *farangs*, who are all determined to outdo one another and make his life ten times more difficult than it should be, and the ever-fun-loving Thais. He now demands the latest stamp issues on letters from abroad and is considering writing a strongly worded letter to his youngest brother about his habit of sending franked mail. It's amazing how these little things take on a sense of outrageous importance when away from home.

The TV programmes are all in Thai and the local cinema only shows Thai films, which means we are stuck when it comes to entertainment. Most people rent videos. Mo flatly refuses to buy a video machine, so we read or go out, but this is year one.

No English magazines are available. However, I have found a small bookshop that sells some English paperbacks and the man who owns it is prepared to try to order if he doesn't have what you want. I find a couple of books that take my fancy and one for Mo. Things are looking up.

Grace, Beth and Cathy go out once a week for lunch and invite me to join them. A couple of weeks later Gina arrives back after a prolonged absence and she now joins us for lunch. We all get on extremely well together and have a good laugh, which is more my style. These women are genuine friends and I realise that this is what makes all the difference. They haven't been thrown together and expected to get on; neither is any hierarchy involved.

Gina is a very funny woman, full of life and passionate about her hotel, which is owned by her husband's family. The pool has improved one hundred per cent since her return and as we have an open invitation to go and use it anytime, Mo and I often have lunch there on a Sunday.

This is the life. A golf lesson at 8am, quick trip to the market, then out to the hotel for a swim, have lunch and then back to the Pile Inn, as we've been calling it since the start of the tourist season, quick shower then go down to Mo's office to help the girls. I now also help Guy, who is setting up an office in town, and Gina when she needs any special typing done. I'm so busy I barely have time for my book. I find a new attraction to add to the list of things to do. Cath has a group of students who are specialising in tourism, and she wants them to practise being tour guides, so Grace, Beth and I are roped in to help.

They all arrive at the hotel by bus at the appointed time and we duly climb on board. Cath introduces us to the students, and we sit down to be model tourists.

They take us to the big *Wat* the first day. When the bus stops, the appointed student tells us where we are, gives a brief talk about it and finishes with 'and now my tourists get off the bus'.

We three are chewing our lips trying not to laugh whilst Cath looks at the girl in horror. 'You have to say please,' she stage-whispers as we are ushered out.

We stand in a group all listening to the appointed tour guide, whose English is remarkably good. Even though we have been there before it's actually very interesting and we find ourselves asking all sorts of questions. Finally, when we have exhausted all the places of interest, we are told by the tour guide to 'get back on the bus'.

'Please!' Cath reminds her pointedly.

I seem to have collected a stack of papers over a number of weeks now and don't like to simply throw them out. When I mention this to Gina she says, 'Oh, Victor will take them for you. He sells them on. He does a lot of work for me. I'll get him to come up and see you. Any job you want done just ask him.'

A couple of days later Victor arrives at the door. He is a likeable Indian gentleman and yes, he will gladly collect the old newspapers from me if I will keep them.

The next week I go up to Grace's apartment early evening before Mo gets back to check on the time for us to meet the next morning for our guided tour. I ring the doorbell and wait. I can hear Grace behind the door, but she isn't opening it for some reason. Finally, it does open but only a crack.

'Yes?' Grace is peering round the edge.

'Hi,' I say, wondering at this strange behaviour.

'Oh, I'm so glad it's you.' She lets out a sigh of relief. 'Come in, quickly.' She pulls the door wide now and ushers me in, closing the door firmly behind her.

'Were you expecting someone else? Where's Beth?'

'She goes over to the hotel most evenings to help Gina. I thought you were the chicken lady,' she says, looking more than a little flustered.

'Who's the chicken lady?'

'Oh, you know how I hate going to the market. Well, I happened to mention it to Gina, and she said she knew the lady who owned the chicken farm, and she would speak to her and arrange for her to deliver a chicken to me.'

'Great.'

'That's what I thought. A couple of nights later someone arrived with a chicken all cleaned and plucked. It was a big chicken and a bit more expensive than I expected, but a whole lot better than going to the market, so I paid the money and put it in the bottom of the fridge.'

'Lucky you, so what's the problem?'

Grace takes a deep breath. 'The problem is that the next night around this time, the doorbell rings and when I open the door the woman is standing there with another chicken that I am supposed to have ordered. I try to tell her that I already have a chicken, but she doesn't understand and gets quite angry, so I had to buy another chicken. I can't cope with any more chicken. This is worse than the quails' eggs.'

We walk into the hotel one day and meet an Englishman who seems to be a bit confused and nervous; he has lost his passport, he says. We suggest all the places it might be and tell him to check his suitcase, but he says he has already looked in all these places so we can only commiserate with him and suggest he asks the manager for help or phones the British consulate in Bangkok. Tourists!

The next day we see him he has found his passport (it was in his suitcase) and all is well.

We meet him again the next week. He seems even more nervous and tells us that he has just been to stay at a National Park for a few days. He was supposed to stay the whole week but left after a rogue elephant apparently flattened one of the wooden houses, killing the couple that were sleeping inside.

Kik hasn't been around for a few days, and I mention this to Victor when he comes to collect the newspapers. 'She has gone for a job interview as a clerk,' he says.

'Oh. Well, I hope she gets the job, but I have to say I'll miss her.'

'Oh, she will be back. She will not get the job.'

'Why not?'

'She has the qualifications, but she does not have the forty thousand baht she will need to buy herself into the job,' he says matter-of-factly.

'What?'

'It is the way it is done. Even the person who wants to work on a building site must have the money to buy themselves into the job.'

'I can't believe it!'

He shrugs his shoulders. 'That is why she works as a maid.'

Grace and Harry have invited us to join them on a trip to Nakhon Ratchasima, Surin and Lopburi. The idea is to see the famous lintel that has just been returned from America and Grace wants to buy some Thai silk.

Chomesri, whose other job seems to be as a tour guide, is organising the trip and on the appointed day we all get into the minibus. Our party consists of Grace and Harry, Chomesri, Chomesri's auntie, a lovely young girl called Kai whom Grace and Harry got to know when they stayed in the hotel where she works in Chiang Rai, and, of course, the driver.

It becomes apparent as the trip goes on that it is important for us all to synchronise our bladders and improve their holding power. At each potential *hong nam* (toilet) stop, Chomesri leaves the bus on her own and marches off to inspect things. We wait and watch with bated breath for her to come back. When she appears, we watch avidly for the signal. A thumbs-up has all those desperate to go inwardly cheering and rushing for relief. In the end you go and squeeze out whatever's there because a thumbs-down means those who are desperate must groan and bear it until the next stop without any guarantees.

Our first night is spent on what feels like an island in the middle of the M1. It's a pleasant hotel but Mo and I can't get to sleep for the noise of the traffic roaring past. It's a relief to get going again the next day. They have no brown bread.

We stop in Lopburi, which, amongst other things, is famous for its population of monkeys. It is necessary to watch bags of any description, food and jewellery, lest these cheeky little creatures decide to help themselves. It's also an excellent place to take children for an explicit introduction to the facts of life: forget the birds and the bees; monkeys are fornicating everywhere.

We finally stop and look at some impressive ruins and see the lintel. The heat is intense now and getting back into the air-conditioned minibus is a welcome retreat.

The next hotel where we are to spend the night has a much better location. We are all having dinner when a woman approaches the table and begins talking to Chomesri. It seems that they are old school friends. She and her family are having dinner at the next table, and it transpires that they plan to spend the weekend at a nearby National Park and we have been invited to stay with them for a night instead of going to a hotel. In fact, they insist on it, so it seems we have no choice. We don't mind; it sounds like fun. Where will we stay? 'Oh, accommodation? *Mai mi pan ha,*' they say with a smile – no problem.

The woman's husband has some prominent position in a local government department, and they are allowed to use these houses in the park at weekends and holidays. There is a golf course, so no one is complaining.

The next day someone remembers that, since we won't be staying at an hotel, there probably won't be any towels, so we make a special trip to a department store to buy some. We drive into the park later and eventually find Chomesri's friends on the golf course. They are still playing but take the time to direct us to some houses at the side of a road going up a hill. The driver stops at a big house on the way up.

Quite a few people seem to be there, and we recognise the woman from last night.

When we get out of the minibus we are invited to go up to the house where the women are busy preparing food. Much discussion is going on and we stand around for a while and then are taken back outside. The next thing is we are taken to a house further down the hill. Kai, Mo and I have gone on ahead. We are shown into the house where we guess we must be staying and have a look round. It has one bedroom with a bed and then a large room with a highly polished wooden floor, but nothing else in it.

Mo and I are beginning to think we should have opted for the hotel. It transpires that the thinking is that Grace and Harry could have the honeymoon suite, meaning the bedroom, and the rest of us could all sleep in the big room. So much for '*mai mee pan ha*'; we should have known.

Luckily, they have a rethink, and we are told to get back into the minibus, which has now arrived with Grace and Harry. We go further down the hill and come to another house where a couple have obviously just sat down outside to enjoy their evening meal. These must be minions, we decide, because a quick discussion ensues, followed by an unhappy-looking couple gathering up their belongings and moving out. We are horrified to think we've put them out of their weekend holiday home but can't say anything for fear of offending Chomesri's friends.

This is finally where we are to stay. We are shown our rooms and told that we have forty minutes to get ready for dinner and please do not be late.

There are seven of us and one bathroom with a toilet and Thai-style shower, which is a small area, blocked off with water in it, which you scoop out and throw over yourself. The water leaves via a drain in the floor.

Like troupers we decide on a rota and each person has an allotted few minutes in which to complete their ablutions. We are all hot and sticky from the day, and Thai people are fastidious about personal hygiene.

Auntie goes first, then Kai, and I am next. It's only when I go in, dressed in a kaftan and clutching my toilet bag, that I realise there is nowhere to put either of them whilst I wash, except an extremely narrow ledge. The floor is already awash with water and I'm running out of thinking time. In the end I roll up my kaftan and hang it round the door handle, then balance the toilet bag on the ledge and pray. The water, of course, is cold – well, tepid.

Somehow, I manage to do everything without getting the kaftan too wet. Mo is next and I rush off to get dressed. Tension is in the air as we are all acutely aware of the passing time. When Grace emerges from the bathroom the intricacies of the whole operation have obviously got to her. She is wandering about looking agitated and confused, saying, 'My glasses, my glasses. I can't find my glasses.' I spot them tightly clutched in her hand and double up laughing. 'Has anyone seen my glasses? I can't find my glasses.' She's getting frantic. I am in tears and trying to point, but she simply thinks I've gone crazy. She turns to Mo, who is equally apoplectic. No matter how hard we try neither of us can get the words out to tell her. My stomach is beginning to ache with all the hilarity, but thankfully Harry appears, realises what's happening, has a laugh and puts her right.

Finally, we are all presentable again. Grace, complete with glasses, can see the funny side of it all now. We present ourselves at the house, where a table is set outside and a huge spread of food has been prepared. All the tension and hysterics have made us hungry. The meal is amazing, a banquet of different dishes and delicious. Of course, as usual, the main attraction for the men, especially the Thai men, is the alcohol, which is being consumed in copious quantities.

During the conversation around the table, it is agreed that the men will all get up at some unearthly hour the next morning to play golf. Grace and I wisely don't volunteer. I am really enjoying this food when I become aware of a silence round the table. I look up and everyone is watching me. 'What's wrong?' I ask Chomesri, who is sitting beside me.

'We're waiting for you to finish,' she says pointedly.

Reluctantly, I put down my fork. It is dark now and it seems that we are all about to go on a tour of the park. The company is quite merry by this time, mainly spurned on by Johnny Walker, who has a lot to answer for in this part of the world.

A large truck arrives, and we are all told to pick up our plastic bucket-seat chairs and take them to this huge lorry, where they are duly hoisted on board. We climb up and claim our seats, which are set out in rows as if we are about to watch a film.

Much drunken hilarity ensues, and I suddenly find myself wondering how the chairs are going to remain in one place, especially as we are about to drive up the remainder of the hill. No one else seems to think this is a problem. I'm still convinced, as we finally get going, that we'll all end up in a pile, but miraculously we reach the top of the hill without the chairs moving. In fact, the way the truck is revving it's a miracle we make it to the top at all.

The object of the exercise is to view the elephants, tigers and other animals at night by spotlight. Of course, the animals can hear us coming a mile away, so they have all taken off, apart from a few startled deer that have probably seen it all before.

The driver is no more sober than anyone else, but somehow, we make it back in one piece.

The house we are in is wooden and basic. Our room is so basic that it has only a bed and a few nails, strategically placed along the bare-wooden wall to hang some clothes on. The mattress on the bed resembles the 'mountains of Mourne', as Mo puts it, and I'm not entirely sure how clean it is. The result is we go to bed with more clothes on than we wore during the day. The electricity goes off at ten o'clock, which is when I get up and open the window and then climb back into bed. Since it's pitch-black and the situation isn't conducive to doing anything else, we concentrate on trying to get to sleep.

After a while we are both still awake. The mattress feels like corrugated cardboard, and I keep feeling itchy, convinced there are bed bugs. A while later Mo is just beginning to drift off when I hear a loud rustling noise in the bushes outside. I suddenly remember our nervous friend from the hotel. My imagination goes into overdrive. Convinced it must be elephants and that the house is in danger of being flattened, I wake Mo.

'Wha?'

'I think I can hear elephants outside.'

Monumental sigh. 'Don't be stupid.'

'Honestly.'

'Well, what do you want me to do about it?'

'Go and look out of the window to check.'

'Why don't you go and check?'

'Because I haven't got my lenses in, so I won't be able to see anything.'

'You can't miss a bloody elephant!'

'Oh, please? Remember what that man told us.'

'Go to sleep.'

'I can't, not now.'

'Tough.'

Now I must get up and go out onto the front porch to look. I can't see anything but then life is a blur without my lenses, so I go back to bed and spend the rest of the night convinced it's our last.

Dawn is announced by the sound of a cockerel accompanied by a lot of loud hawking and spitting as our neighbours prepare themselves for the new day.

Mo climbs slowly out of bed, deeply regretting that he agreed to such an early start, but if he and Harry want any breakfast they must be up at the house at the appointed time. It's impossible to snuggle down in this bed, so I get up, shower after Mo and Harry have left, and read a book for a while until the others are ready.

Grace, Chomesri, Auntie, Kai and I all make our way up to the big house for breakfast. It transpires that Chomesri and her aunt were so upset at the accommodation that they spent several hours meditating before they could get to sleep.

It's a beautiful morning and we sit outside at a long wooden table. When breakfast arrives, it is a bowl of rice porridge with a side dish of pickles and slices of hard-boiled egg. Grace is horrified. 'Oh my, do they have any coffee? I'll just have coffee.' There isn't any. Kai and Auntie are tucking in; Chomesri is in the house.

'Maybe it won't be so bad,' I say, and we both take a spoonful.

Grace swallows some and puts the spoon down. 'I can't eat this stuff, it's tasteless.'

It's also tepid by this time and, I have to admit, not palatable.

'I think the pickles are meant to give it some taste,' I say, hesitating to try.

'No. I couldn't. I just want a cup of coffee,' Grace says. 'I'll be fine if I can just have some coffee.' Whereupon Chomesri arrives and informs us that she must go and buy a film somewhere if we'd like to go with her.

Sure that this means that we'll be able to get some coffee, we climb into the back of the car she has borrowed. Chomesri is focused on a new roll of film. We are desperate for a cup of coffee, which we might have got there, we think, as we drive past a potential source by way of a hotel in the park. Chomesri eventually gets her film. Grace and I by this time would kill for a coffee but again we sail past the hotel on the way back. 'We'd just like a coffee,' we say at last in desperation, but too late: Chomesri is now focused on getting the car back to its owner on time. We have to settle for water.

Later we meet up with everyone again. Chomesri's friend is not amused her husband hit a cracking shot; unfortunately, she was ahead of him and got in the way of the ball. Probably just as well we are leaving.

Our last night we are able to stay in a real hotel again. This one has shops. I spot a life-sized cloth-stuffed parrot for Mo's birthday and Grace agrees to keep it for me until then. Mo and I revel in the luxury of a hot shower and a comfortable, king-sized bed with clean, starched sheets. Next morning, when we go down for breakfast, Grace is happily tucking into eggs, toast and a pot full of coffee.

CHAPTER ELEVEN

The latest news is that the army is coming to town. It seems that Pits is to host a joint exercise between the Thai and American forces. In past times Gina has been roped in as a voluntary translator, organiser of laundry and other necessities, counsellor and substitute mother who is willing to organise things that their own mothers wouldn't want to know about. This time she is determined she is going to make some money out of it.

I am roped in to help by typing out a tender to supply certain items that will be needed. This is when I find out that Gina's office hours are anything but normal and I end up over at the hotel with her and Beth until 2am typing out this bloody tender. My next assignment is to persuade Guy, who mustn't know about it, to let me use his fax machine in his new office, which has not yet opened for such business. A bit of subterfuge is required, and with Beth lending support and me lying through my teeth, eventually the deed is done.

Rumour has it that Guy is also putting in a bid that Gina isn't supposed to know about. A drink in the pub becomes a decidedly dicey business. Talk is of nothing else but these exercises and how much money everyone is going to make. I try not to put my foot in it by giving anything away. It's all highly stressful.

A captain and his team have now arrived to prepare for the influx of soldiers taking part in the exercises. They are staying at Gina's hotel, and she is doing her best to help them out.

One of the men on Gina's staff at the hotel is set on becoming a woman and saving up madly for the operation. It's quite difficult to tell he isn't yet a woman, and Gina, who feels sorry for him, does everything she can to boost his confidence.

I arrive one evening and see Gina at the top of the steps leading up to the hotel. She is grinning and waving to someone who has just got into a taxi. Apparently, it's one of the forces guys going out on a date. Gina is wondering how long it will take him to realise that his date, with whom he is besotted, isn't a woman.

I hear the next day that when he did find out his reaction was to beat up his so-called buddies who had known but hadn't told him. It seems that drinks got thrown and glass was broken; Gina, however, remains miraculously unscathed.

We have finally decided to move into the small house with the swimming pool. In the absence of anyone else showing an interest in renting his house, apart from an Indian couple who have just arrived in town, Khun Choochai has agreed to paint the walls.

The Pile Inn staff are quite upset that we are leaving; the owner has even instructed Khun Pornsak to reduce our rent, but he can't do anything about the tourists. The *Wat* across the way still needs money and we desperately need some sleep. The noise from the *Wat* is like having the TV on full blast in the apartment. I keep thinking we should close the doors but then realise they are already shut. Add to that the monkey whoop-whooping all day and it's enough to drive anyone crazy. Time to move on. Thank goodness Khun Choochai agreed to paint.

It's Mo's birthday and Grace kindly decides to prepare a birthday meal for him in the evening. We have a drink whilst he opens his presents. He loves his parrot and Grace has given him a baseball cap. I take a photograph of him wearing it and holding the parrot. Grace has made tacos with all the trimmings, which we haven't had before so it's a real treat.

We have now booked our flights to go back home on leave. We've decided to visit Mo's brother in New York on the way home and will fly to San Francisco first. It seems that we need a visa for the States and since Gina is friendly with the guy in the consulate in Chiang Mai, this is where we go for our next R&R.

Unfortunately, this time of year is the hottest part of the dry season, and our visit will coincide with the Thai New Year Songkran festival. Aroon is ecstatic for us. 'Songkran Chiang Mai, number one, madame. Oh.' He shakes his head as if he can't believe our luck. I am less enthusiastic. For the uninitiated, it seems that an ancient tradition, whereby the younger members of the family paid respect to the elder members and friends by pouring a little water over the palms of their hands, has now got totally out of control. Nowadays it's very much a free-for-all with everyone throwing water at anyone passing by. It goes on for three or four days, so unless you want to get soaked it's advisable to stay indoors. Some of the water, it seems, is mixed with perfumed talcum powder, and it stains. I decide to take my raincoat.

When we arrive in Chiang Mai it's like driving onto a film set. Everyone is going crazy. The streets are lined with people young and old, absolutely soaked to the skin, filling buckets from the river that runs through the town and throwing water everywhere. The main targets are people on motorbikes, open trucks, tuk-tuks or *samlors*; in other words, anyone who is exposed, although the cars also get their fair share if they forget to lock their doors. Ours are hastily dealt with.

Groups of Thais patrol the streets in the back of trucks, with huge water barrels, and throw water at everyone as they go along. It's all done in a spirit of good fun; no one can get angry or object, but it can be very dangerous, we see, as a motorbike skids and falls to the ground in front of us. The saving grace is that everything stops in the evening, presumably so that the night market can continue undisturbed.

We have worked out a plan. We couldn't get into the hotel we normally stay in on the first night, so we have booked into another hotel for one night. The room obviously hasn't been used for a while by humans, but several families of mosquitoes seem to have taken up residence and our first half hour is spent smacking them against the wall. These little bastards of the insect world and I have one thing in common: we are particularly partial to Mo's body, so they have to go.

We shower and change, and since everywhere seems to be full, we eat in a restaurant on the main drag, where the night market takes place. As we sit waiting for our food to come, we realise, too late, that a large party is having a meal at the far end of the room, and they have brought their children along. This time there is no nanny, and the kids are running riot. For some reason no one will tackle these little demons. The waiters only smile indulgently and walk on past.

We notice that a well-spoken Englishman is sitting at a table near us also waiting for his meal. He calls the waiter across and in a loud voice asks him to do something about the children who are running around, completely oblivious to the fact that anyone else is in the room. The waiter smiles, says, 'Yes, sir,' and walks away. There is some discussion, but no one does anything, and I have to say, sticking my foot out to trip the little buggers up is sorely tempting.

Our food arrives, but the man is still waiting. The kids have now gone up to the other end of the restaurant to regroup. They launch their next assault and come tearing round the English gentleman's table, whereupon he gets up and marches out past the astonished waiter now bearing his food. We are filled with admiration and only hope that he wasn't too hungry.

The next day we go to the American consulate to collect our visa. Thankfully, it is in a quieter part of town, but I wear my raincoat just in case, then realise why people don't tend to wear raincoats: it's the equivalent of zipping yourself into a portable sauna. The consulate turns out to be a bit of a walk from where we are parked. I am parboiled by the time we get to the place and highly relieved once the visas have been handed over by Gina's nice American friend and we reach the safety of the car again.

When we move to the better hotel, we decide that if we are going to get wet it might as well be in the swimming pool. We pick a couple of loungers and park ourselves for the rest of the day, watching the antics of an English family of rather genteel skinheads who seem to have a penchant for earrings, the men more so than the women.

By six o'clock all is quiet again and we do the rounds of the night market. I buy a pair of attractive mules in a woven dark brown basket-like material, which miraculously are my size, and then later go back and buy a black pair. We also stock up on T-shirts to take home as presents.

The next day we are leaving and walk down to the hotel shopping area, congratulating ourselves on having managed to stay dry for the whole visit. I buy a couple of postcards, and as we begin to walk back along the path leading into the hotel, we are confronted with a small boy pointing a water pistol at us. I give him my 'don't you dare' look, which obviously doesn't translate into Thai because we are both given a good squirt, which he thinks is outrageously funny. Little bugger.

Back in Pits we discover that Grace and Harry didn't get off so lightly. Having lived at the hotel before, they are much loved by all the staff. Apparently, they were soaked several times in town, and then later, when they had got dried off, the manager lured them out to the back of the hotel where the staff had congregated, and they were invited to sit down whilst each employee took a turn to pour water over them. They just had to laugh and pretend to enjoy it. Beth, it seems, was gently lowered into the swimming pool at Gina's hotel. Boy, are we glad we went to Chiang Mai!

We pay another visit to the house, which has now been painted and looks much better. All the old wallpaper has gone, and the walls are now a creamy colour, which sets off the dark wooden floors and makes the place look much bigger. A new dining table sits in the space under the stairway, and we tell Khun Choochai that, as we have our own settee, we won't be needing his grey fake leather one with the broken leg, although it's touch and go as to whether it is more spine-torturing than the one we have.

One more thing that grates a lot is the highly polished wooden seat, which is taking up the whole outside patio and which appears to have been fashioned from the bottom of a huge tree with roots still intact. This back-breaking monstrosity is taking up the space I need for a table and chairs and where I have visions of writing letters and enjoying coffee and drinks with friends. Too taken up with the concerns re the painting, this has hitherto not been mentioned, so I decide to take the plunge. Khun Choochai thinks it will be too heavy to move but he will speak to his wife about it, which doesn't bode well for a positive outcome.

We are taken across to his house, which is much bigger than ours. It has the same dark wooden floors and also has a tiled area with a sink in the living room. At the back of the room are our new mattresses still wrapped in plastic to show that they are new, a double one for our room upstairs and two singles for the beds in the guest room.

'Is it OK with you if we don't put the two smaller mattresses in straight away? If you are going to UK soon it would be better to leave the beds downstairs with no mattress, in case somebody goes in there to sleep.'

'Of course, but why would somebody go in?' I ask cautiously.

'It is OK, just a precaution,' he says, so we agree.

Our only worry now is that Khun Choochai has several dogs – seven, to be exact, three of them being large Alsatians, one small white dog and the others some curious mixture. They are all barking menacingly from their kennels in the background. Mo is wary of dogs, especially Alsatians, having been bitten by one when he was a child. Khun Choochai assures us that he only lets them out at night for security.

Whilst we appreciate the security aspect, we don't want to get out of the car late in the evening to find ourselves confronted with a pack of dogs that might not understand the finer points of renting and consider us to be a security risk. Khun Choochai, who was educated in America and speaks fluent English, laughs and assures us this will not be a problem. 'As long as you don run.' I wonder how on earth he can be so sure, but having no suitable alternative, we say we'll move in next week.

Gina, who speaks fluent Thai, has kindly taken a great interest in all of this and offers to have some of her staff move our goods and chattels into the new house.

We go down the night before the big move to take some boxes with dishes for the kitchen. It is dark, but thankfully the dogs are still locked up, which is just as well as Mo has to fumble around trying to get the key into the lock. Once inside, we go through the lounge area to get to the kitchen at the back. Mo switches on the light. I kneel in front of one of the cupboards and then let out a scream as I suddenly realise a huge dark brown cockroach is running up my arm. I am frozen with fear. Mo, in biology teacher mode, informs me it's a flying cockroach. Whereupon I, in hysterical panic mode, yell that I don't care what kind of fucking cockroach it is, will he please just get it off me.

The next day is moving day and Mo, of course, has to disappear off to work. Luckily, the lunch bunch all turn up to help with the final packing. Gina has arranged for some of the men from her hotel to bring a large truck. I had envisioned a van but don't like to comment. We have already taken down quite a few boxes and there still seems to be a lot to move. Under Gina's watchful eye, the company furniture is carefully loaded on to the truck along with all the other bits and pieces, and the last thing to go is a large floppy green plant.

Any hopes of doing this discreetly are totally banished, I realise, when we all go downstairs to see the truck off. It turns right out of the hotel car park, piled up with all our worldly goods and Gina perched on top of the drinks fridge, one hand clutching our large green plant and the other held high, pointing forth like Boadicea leading her troops into battle. Unfortunately, the house is on the outskirts of the town at the opposite end from the hotel so everyone in Pits will know about our move.

By the time I get down there, two of Gina's maids have miraculously appeared and she is busy directing them as to where everything should go. I am almost surplus to requirements and nearly forget for a moment that I am the one moving in. It's all done amazingly quickly so that by the time they have finished there isn't a cardboard box in sight and the place looks like we have been living in it forever.

I produce a bottle of Mekhong, and Gina and I settle ourselves down in the kitchen whilst the maids are duly dispatched to watch TV in the lounge area. I can't thank her enough. I'm still amazed, but she shrugs it off and has another Mekhong. When Mo arrives much later, he walks into the lounge, finds the two maids watching TV and thinks he has got the wrong house until he reaches the kitchen and is greeted by two grinning females whom he does recognise and who by this time are quite tipsy.

'I thought I'd got the wrong house,' he informs us. 'I was expecting to be met with cardboard boxes all over the place.'

'Well, it's all down to Gina and her maids,' I tell him. 'They did all the work, just had to tell them where to put everything.' This, I realise as I say it, is a bit of a fib, because Gina had taken charge and I seem to remember hoping I'd be able to find everything once they have gone.

Although we are sharing a maid with the property owner next door, she will only be doing the cleaning, washing and ironing. I still do the shopping and cooking. Tonight, we eat out but can't believe our luck that we don't have to face any unpacking when we get back.

That night we crawl into our new bed with new mattress, in our huge bedroom, and fall into a blissful sleep until I have to get up to go to the loo in the middle of the night in the dark and fall over the bloody rowing machine.

The next morning is strange as we adjust to the new house. I am up and showered first, ready to go to the market as soon as Aroon gets back from taking Mo to the office. We sit at the little kitchen table with its bent leg, having our muesli and telling each other that this is much better.

Aroon arrives all smiles, obviously relieved not to have to run the gauntlet of the tourists to get to the hotel. No more parking problems, so we can see him arriving, which makes a big difference, and he can have a seat and a quick fag on the patio.

The only thing is that if I want to go anywhere I either have to rely on Aroon or get a tuk-tuk. Gone are the days when I can wander down at my leisure, but then you can't have everything, and we do have a pool in the back garden.

It is now extremely hot and poor Mo is having to work hard and not getting back until late. As a result, he is too tired to be bothered doing anything in the evening.

The washing machine and dryer must go into the downstairs bathroom, but the washing machine isn't connected yet, so Mook the maid has to wash our clothes by hand using the two-basin method. I have gathered up the clothes and given them to her. Several minutes later Khun Wipa, the landlord's wife, arrives at the door. I haven't a clue what she's on about, so she leads me to where Mook is busy doing the washing. I still don't understand until Mook holds up a pair of Mo's underpants. 'You wan Mook wash?' she asks, with a strange look on her face. Puzzled by this, I can only think to say yes, wondering why she should ask. She seems incredulous but tells the maid to carry on.

Later in the afternoon, when Mook appears to do the ironing, I don my bikini, put a robe on and go for a quick swim in the pool.

It is enclosed by a high-wire fence but not hidden from the rest of the garden. No one is around and I swim up and down, savouring the chance to get some real exercise without having to avoid other bodies. After a while I can feel my skin beginning to pucker. At this point a somewhat emaciated-looking man arrives on the scene and starts spraying some bushes just on the other side of the fence. His skin is a deep nut brown. This must be Sunti the gardener.

Acutely aware of Thai sensitivities to exposed flesh, I hover in the pool treading water to delay my inevitable exposure, hoping against hope that he will go away before I begin to resemble a piece of raw tripe. He is in no hurry, so I must tread water until he eventually turns his back to do something, and I can make a quick dash for my towel.

Later in the pub, the pop-up version of *Encyclopaedia Britannica* (anything you need to know just ask; everyone will have an opinion), I am informed that the wife is supposed to wash her husband's underpants.

The washing machine is connected the next day, so the problem is solved. Mook is ecstatic. I challenge Khun Choochai later about buying his wife a washing machine. He is a very rich man, I tell him, why doesn't he buy one? But it falls on deaf ears and poor Mook still has to do their washing by hand.

An invitation comes via word of mouth to go to the oil company compound for drinks on Friday night at six o'clock. In an effort to improve relationships amongst themselves and with the rest of us, they have been told to fraternise. They are expected to take it in turns to host the evening. I dread it, but politeness dictates that we must go.

It's in the country manager's house. Not that the actual house makes any difference because they are all the same, I realise, when we walk in, apart from the furnishings, that is. I am instantly on the lookout for the monk. Everyone is going out of their way to be politely friendly; I'm even offered some bread from a newly ordered batch by one of the wives. We all stand around stiffly making polite conversation.

A couple of drinks later, I am standing opposite Mo at a table set with various small eats. I look across at him and smile; he grins back and, judging by the glazed look in his eye I realise that although he hasn't had much to drink, the person pouring has a heavy hand and Mo hasn't eaten anything since lunchtime. Horrified, I check no one is looking and mouth to him that he has had too much gin. He merely grins back. I wait for another chance and try again, but he only looks puzzled. I try to mouth to him to eat something quick, thinking at this rate he'll be pie-eyed and legless before the next hour is up.

He isn't catching on, so in desperation, eyes still on him, I pointedly pick up something from the nearest plate and deliberately widen my eyes as I put it into my mouth. Too late I realise it's one of those bloody awful cocktail sausages I can't stand. In the end I am forced to make my way round to where he is standing, pick up a bite-sized pastry thing, tell him he's pissed without moving my lips and, with an endearing smile, guide it into his mouth.

After a while, a young couple arrive with a toddler in tow. These are the people who let us off the hook by moving into the big house we weren't keen on. We are introduced. The woman's name is Judy, her husband is Rob and their daughter is called Chloe. They seem genuinely nice, but everyone is being very polite. There's something about the atmosphere that seems so contrived.

Later we get a chance to chat, find we have an instant rapport, and Judy and I arrange to meet for a coffee.

Judy is good fun; we share a lot of interests and opinions. We laugh about the food, and I tell her about my baked potatoes. 'With me it was omelettes,' she says, grinning. 'I stuffed them with everything I could think of, but now we settle for Thai food. Luckily, the maid is a great cook. I just leave everything to her and she's great with Chloe.'

The weekly lunch is coming up, so I invite Judy along and introduce her to the others. Not surprisingly, everyone takes to her.

The weather is particularly hot these days, so much so that a swim in the pool, to which I am now addicted, is like taking a warm bath. Wiser now, I leave my towel right at the edge of the pool. On my way back from my swim I notice Sunti, who we have since discovered only has one eye, poor man, stretched out fast asleep on the path between the two houses. Poor soul must be tired, out working in this heat.

There's a birthday celebration at the pub tonight, but Mo is late getting back. I am tempted not to wake him when he falls asleep after his usual plate of fruit and a cup of tea, he looks so tired. However, he wakes up on his own and pronounces himself refreshed.

The place is crowded when we arrive. By this time, we know so many people, both *farangs* and Thais, that everyone is calling out hello as we walk in. The oil company people, who are all there, give us a funny look as if they can't believe we know so many people. We find a seat at the bottom end of the bar and order our drinks. After a few minutes, Frances's husband comes round and sits down on a stool beside us. He's very chatty and then says, 'Well, now that we've got Rob and Judy fixed up with a membership to the club, we'll have to see about getting memberships for you two.'

He's referring to the club at the condominium. There always has been a verbal agreement allowing us to use it, but we don't push the point. Instead, I tell him it won't be necessary because now we have our own swimming pool. I think he can tell by the tone of my voice that I am not much taken with his belated efforts at being friendly.

He goes on to explain that they all have great expectations when it comes to their living accommodation and recreational facilities. 'We have come to expect a certain standard,' he says, 'and it's annoying when something is missing.' Of course, he's referring to the bloody squash court again, but I suppose if you're used to living at a certain level that's that. At least he's making the effort now.

Word has got round that we are going on leave in a few weeks. When I go to collect my rolls, the baker tackles me.

'You go UK?'

'Yes.'

'You know helmeh for motobie?'

'Yes,' I say warily; there is rumour about making it compulsory for motorcyclists to wear helmets.

'I ask Khun Monique to get one for me from France but she say no can get. UK have?'

I am mentally trying to fit a crash helmet into our case, and it just won't shut. 'Eh, no, we go Scotland, I no think Scotland have,' I lie badly. There's a limit to what you can do for people. Mo has already been asked to find a spare part for an old car.

Aroon parks the car in the tree-lined street in front of the office; we are here to pick Mo up to go for lunch. He turns round in his seat and grins. 'Madame know Ka shoes?'

'Ka shoes?' What on earth is he talking about?

'Yes, madame, number one.'

I haven't a clue. 'Ka shoes.' This is a real puzzle. We're in a hurry and he is obviously preoccupied with these bloody shoes because he switches off the engine, locks me in the car and goes into the company building to phone Mo from reception. He's gone a lot longer than I thought he would be and it's getting hotter by the second. I try to open the windows, but they are automatic, and I can't figure out any way to do it and the back seat has childproof locks. I'm almost at panic stage when he reappears. He opens the driver's door. 'Open this door, Aroon. Too hot. You shut off AC,' I say, too relieved to see him to be angry.

'Very sorry, madame,' he says, as I leap out into the comparatively fresh air. I lean against the door, savouring the slight breeze and the chance to cool down and breathe again whilst we wait. Across the road is a small outdoor restaurant where people are busily eating. 'Ka shoes, Aroon. I no understand.'

'Same same Nike, Adidas, madame. Ka shoes. Number one, madame, number one,' he says with religious conviction. 'My fren bring from Saudi Arabia, but wrong sie.'

Now I'm even more puzzled, but I've got the message: he wants us to bring him back a pair of shoes and this time we'll have to oblige.

I ask Mo about it when we go up to the hotel for lunch. They do a wonderful buffet and we're addicted to their red curry with rice, so whenever Mo is in the office at lunchtime, which isn't often, we go there to eat.

It's payday for the army and the coffee shop is heavy with smoke coming from a table filled with inebriated colonels or whatever rank they are. Max, who goes in every day for his lunch, waves as we sit down at our table. The smoke and the heavy tones from the singer make for a languid mood.

Mo is as puzzled as I am when I tell him about the Ka shoes; we try hard to connect it with something but have to give up in the end.

Next morning Aroon arrives with a pair of soft desert boots. They are made by Clarks. He was talking about Clarks shoes. At least they should fit into the suitcase.

Mook is looking coy and dreamy, I notice, when I go upstairs to get something from the bedroom. 'Madame go UK?' She is slowly dusting one of the glass shelves, her cloth hovering around my bottle of Chanel No 5. 'This good, madame?'

'Yes, very good, very expensive, Khun Mo give me for present.'

'Mook like,' she says, smiling. 'I give money, madame can buy for Mook?'

Bloody hell!

I am in two minds about going back on leave. Since we have only just moved to the house, I don't feel the need to get away. Mo, however, feels differently. He has really been working hard and badly needs a break away from it all. His daily dealings with the oil company are difficult. He must tell them things they don't want to know, and he is pig in the middle between two rival departments. Thank goodness we have made some friends who are not involved with his work.

Grace and Harry are a godsend, especially when Mo and I fall out about something. We usually end up going to visit them. They are always pleased to see us and so cheerful. After an hour in their company, a couple of Harry's stiff whiskies for Mo and Grace's lethal vodka lime tonics for me, plus a few handfuls of salted peanuts, all is right with the world again. They are marvellous. I wonder what they do when they have an argument.

We often follow an impromptu visit by going out for a meal together, usually to the restaurant beside the hotel. Don't know its real name but Mo has christened it Mama Sans. Grace and Harry are friendly with the woman whose family owns it and the food is really good.

One night Beth joins us, and we order several different dishes to share as usual. I love this way of eating. You don't have a whole plate of food to finish but merely help yourself to whatever you fancy. The food is prepared based on a small amount of protein, e.g., chicken meat or fish, usually cooked with vegetables and always eaten with rice. It's a much healthier way to eat.

We order some beers and wait for the food. I have now developed a taste for beer in the absence of wine almost everywhere we go. This time we have ordered what are called one-hundred-year-old eggs, just to try. They prove to be quite palatable, and the discussion begins as to how they are prepared. Of course, they can't be one hundred years old. In the end we call the owner over, tell her we've enjoyed the meal and enquire about the eggs. How do they preserve them?

'Horse's urine,' is the reply. We hope perhaps she has misunderstood the question and, for the sake of everyone's digestion, deem it to be one of those things it's better not to know.

CHAPTER TWELVE

We go to the pub and find that the atmosphere is decidedly tense. Guy, it seems, was not successful in his bid to tender for the army exercises. He has found out that Gina also put in a bid and failed but blames her for the whole thing going wrong. They are no longer friends. I sit quietly sipping my drink, admitting to nothing and looking suitably concerned. Mo does the same.

Not to be outdone, Gina decides to make her money by setting up shop on the army campsite. She takes herself off to Bangkok on a buying spree and comes back laden with T-shirts, socks, shorts, pants, fake big-name brands, of course, plus watches and all the other touristy stuff. A cousin of Jake's comes up from Bangkok to sell gold.

In the meantime, the Thai army wives have also decided to get in on the act and have the clout to monopolise, so all those who thought like Gina now find themselves banned from the camp.

Ever a trouper, Gina sets up shop in the hotel instead, and when she tells us what she paid for everything I wonder if the poor people who make these things get any money at all.

Word has got round, and the female population of Pits has increased over the weeks; there seem to be women everywhere.

'They're on the game.' Mo nods towards two women sitting at a table nearby as we are having dinner in the coffee shop at Gina's hotel.

'How do you know that?'

'You can tell.'

'How?'

'Look at them.'

'I am.'

'Look at the way they're dressed. It's obvious.'

'Is it?'

How does he know so much? I wonder.

As well as Mui, they have a new barmaid in the pub now called Pet and a *farang* gentleman we haven't met before called Arthur. Arthur retired from his job in the UK several years before and married the Thai lady sitting beside him. Her name is Madee. Pet is Madee's grown-up daughter. Arthur, now in his seventies, is happily enjoying his retirement years in Thailand, he tells us. Best thing he ever did, he says.

As well as the shop, Gina has also decided to set up an audition to find a group plus singer to play at the disco in the basement of the hotel. Unfortunately, the local talent is not up to the standard she requires so she decides to look further afield. After a drink too many in the bar one evening, she somehow manages to rope me into going talent-spotting with her and Beth.

This must be done at night and by the time the appointed evening arrives, I am not at all sure that it's a good idea. I become even more convinced when Gina and Beth pick me up at the house and I discover (once we are on our way) that Jake has insisted that Gina carry a gun with her. Apparently, he told Gina that three women on their own need protection, which to me does not bode well for the night to come. To make matters worse, I have an uncanny feeling about the whole thing.

We drive for what seems like miles and miles through pitch-blackness and end up in a small bar where a waitress with an extremely deep voice asks what we would like to drink. '*Katoy*,' Gina whispers when he goes off to get the drinks. This place is basic and verging on seedy to me so I'm more than happy when it turns out that the group and singers here are not much good, and we can go on to another place.

Eventually we end up in a hotel God knows where. The reception area is huge, and we seem to be the only people there. Hungry now and badly in need of some ballast to soak up the drinks we've had, we decide to have something to eat. We go into the almost empty restaurant and Gina orders her favourite dish, which she urges us to try. It turns out to be some kind of sausage made from raw pork, which I have had before and tastes OK.

'I shouldn't really be eating this,' Gina says, scratching her arm as Beth and I are chewing away busily. 'If you eat too much of it, you can get a parasite that lies underneath your skin. It itches like shit,' she says, scrubbing hard. 'It's supposed to go away after a few years,' she informs us, still scratching. 'I practically lived on the stuff when I first came here. People kept telling me not to eat so much of it, but I was hooked.'

Beth and I stop chewing as the story penetrates. 'You have to eat a lot of it,' Gina says by way of reassurance. A masticated ball of the stuff is now sitting at the back of my tongue waiting to begin its digestive journey. I decide I'll quietly get rid of it. A waiter appears and begins to pour water into the glasses. I don't want any ice. In the rush to tell him, reflex action takes over and I discover I have swallowed the offending ball by mistake. Oh well.

Gina finishes the remainder of the sausage, and we go into the hall, where the resident group for this month is playing. They are from Malaysia, four men and a woman. The woman, who is the singer, is particularly good. At last, this is the kind of talent Gina has been looking for, thank God, and after they have finished singing, she arranges to hire them as soon as possible.

Relieved that we can now go back home, we climb into the car and heave a great sigh. This is short-lived, however, as it becomes patently obvious that Gina doesn't know how to get out of town. No matter which road she takes, we keep ending up at the same place again. This goes on for ages. We seem to be doomed to stay in this town forever. Time is rushing by, and Mo is waiting up to let me in as Khun Choochai locks the big gates every night and they must be opened from a special switch across at his house. Sunti usually does it but doesn't always wake up if it is late. Grace and Harry will be worried about Beth, and Jake was uneasy about the whole idea to start with.

Gina has one last try and then finally parks, marches into a bar and eventually comes out with two men, who get into the car with us. Beth and I think she has finally taken leave of her senses until she explains that she offered a hundred baht to anyone who would show us the way out of town and these two guys agreed. Luckily the two men do not turn out to be serial rapists (just as well since the gun is shut in the glove compartment) and when we are finally on the right road, she thanks them, hands over the money and lets them out of the car.

We get back after 1am by which time Mo has fallen asleep on the couch so we spend ages pressing the buzzer until he finally opens the gate.

The Pile Inn has a massage parlour on the fourth floor, which I have never been to; neither, I hope, has Mo. Gina's hotel also has a massage parlour. The women all sit in some kind of window and while away their time crocheting and knitting whilst they wait for their clients to come in. It seems, from what Gina is saying, that not all the women are genuine massage therapists. 'So how do you tell which is which?' I enquire, in the interest of research.

'Look for the one with the longest piece of knitting,' she says with a throaty laugh. 'She's the real thing.'

'You mean there's only one?' By way of reply, Gina digs her chin down into her neck and gives another throaty laugh.

The army have begun to arrive. Every business in town is convinced it is going to make a fortune, but Gina knows better. 'Their per diem isn't that much and they are only going to be allowed into town in batches, so it looks like the army wives will stand to make the most money, but we'll see.' She sounds philosophic, but knowing her she'll have something up her sleeve.

Mimi is busy trying to persuade all the best-looking girls in town to start spending their evenings in the pub. Gina wants them to come to her hotel to help entertain the officers; it's all getting a bit fraught for the girls, who do not want to fall out with either of them. 'I don' know what to do,' Chim, who works at the local travel agency, tells me. I have been helping Gina and now need a lift down to Mo's office but none of the hotel cars are available. 'I take you,' Chim says, sitting on her motorbike, and in a moment of madness I agree to go.

Oh God, why did I do this? I wail silently as we weave in and out of the traffic. Sitting astride the back seat, holding on to Chim, trying not to panic and terrified I'll lose my balance. There is no way I can assume the nonchalant air of the Thai women perched side-saddle on the back of other bikes that pass by. I am aware of being a clumsy *farang* and wish I could simply disappear. When we finally come to a halt outside the office building, I quickly dismount and thank her, vowing never to get on a motorbike again.

When we walk into the pub one night, we see that, not to be left out, Pet's mother Madee has commandeered her own group and the place is full of strange women. The pub has lost its cosy family feeling, which results in much consternation amongst the regulars. 'Have to wait to get a bloody drink these days,' Max complains bitterly. Mimi, on the other hand, is walking around grinning like a Cheshire cat.

Things are going well at our new abode. Khun Choochai's canine pack, whilst not responding to 'good doggies', stand back and watch with interest as we leave the car and, mindful of Khun Choochai's advice, walk at a calculated slow pace towards our house. Fortunately, it's only a short distance, which doesn't give the pack instinct time to manifest.

Mook comes in every day late morning to clean and do the washing and then comes back later to do the ironing in the afternoon. I am seriously into Thai food these days and go to the market most mornings with Aroon. Judy comes down for a coffee every now and then, and the lunch bunch meet once a week at a different venue.

Golf lessons continue. I have graduated to the putting green now and such is my prowess that Khun Charong has taken to spending almost the entire lesson standing at the side of the green reading a comic and picking his nose. Every so often he will glance up and say curtly, 'Yes, madame, good, good,' or, 'Again, again,' and seems highly put out if he is forced to abandon his tome to correct my mistakes. Like an old married couple unsuited from the start, we are rapidly tiring of each other.

Khun Wipa has been across a few times for a friendly 'chat'. It's obvious that she has taken great delight in telling her rival, the colonel's wife, that we have moved in. The colonel's wife now has Judy, whom the colonel takes a great interest in, plus Rob and Chloe, so she can't really complain. Still, I get the impression Khun Wipa reckons she got one over on her rival.

Judy tells me that some mornings she has taken to spending an hour in the little hotel cafe drinking Blue Mountain coffee and enjoying the peace and quiet to smoke one of her rollups and read the paper. Chloe now attends the local Thai nursery school not far from the house. Judy is also in the enviable position of having inherited a wonderful maid, who does everything, including the daily shopping and cooking. Lucky cow! They also inherited the hunky-looking gardener. *Now, if Sunti were younger and looked like him then I could really get going on my book*, I think, as I step over his prostrated body on the path. He is sound asleep. God, that poor man must be tired.

In the meantime, I am determined to cook proper Thai food and, being me, everything must be authentic. My red and green curry pastes are made from scratch with all the right ingredients bought fresh from the market. It takes some time, but I want it to be just like the locals eat it. Mook views all of this with eagle-eyed interest as she bobs down and passes through the kitchen. This habit of cowering down as if I am about to hit her every time she passes me, I find really irritating. However, it is supposed to be a sign of respect and is what she has been taught to do, so I bite my tongue.

It's a curry day again and I go through the painstaking process of making the curry paste as usual. Mook comes and goes, ducking past me with a quiet smile, her eyes carefully noting everything I am doing.

She must have given her daily report back to headquarters because a little later Khun Wipa arrives at the back door clutching a small red parcel. 'Mook tell me you make,' she says, pointing to the red curry paste in the blender. 'Same same this.' She holds up the parcel of red paste. 'Can buy *hah* [five] baht from maket.' She laughs.

Judy is looking perkier than normal when she next comes down for a coffee. 'I was in the little cafe yesterday having my usual Blue Mountain and these guys came in.' Her eyes are sparkling as she sits down.

Uh oh. 'Just a minute,' I say, rushing off to get the coffee. This is not to be missed.

'One of them was really nice,' she says, daintily licking along the gummed line of her newly rolled cigarette. 'He kept looking at me and then he came across and asked if I minded him joining me.' My ears are on high alert as I pour the coffee into her cup. 'It was so good to be able to have an interesting conversation with a man again.' She sips her coffee with a far-off look. I feel myself tense. Rob is away. She sighs. 'He and his friends were only here for the day.' My shoulders drop with relief. She's too good-looking to be left on her own.

'Want one?' she asks, nodding towards the packet of tobacco. Definitely!

Gina's hotel is obviously popular with the army and air force officers; they are swarming around everywhere, men and women, and she is doing her best to keep everybody entertained and happy.

Her new business is prospering. Beth is helping, assisted by two of Gina's maids, May and Nit. All goes well until Beth introduces May to Burmese cheroots. Gina is furious because her apartment now 'stinks like shit'. I go in one afternoon to help. Not much is happening so I pick up a magazine that May has been reading and almost gag at the picture of a dead body covered in blood. The whole magazine is filled with similar pictures of victims of crime scenes and accidents. 'Thai people love this kind of thing,' Beth tells me when I show her. Ugh!

The next night we go to the pub. It's like a different place, packed out with strange women and soldiers with wall-to-wall shoulders sitting along the bar. These guys are enormous. Max is standing knocking his empty glass on the bar and muttering under his breath. 'You ought to be able to do something about this,' he derides Theo.

'How?' Theo's glassy eyes look stunned.

'You've got a bloody share in the place.'

'You're right, so I have.' He holds his glass up commandingly. 'Hey, Mui. I've got shares in this place. Put another one in there, please.' Mui is busy answering a call at the other end of the bar. 'Doesn't make any bloody difference,' Theo mutters, placing his empty glass back down again.

'They're just ignoring us regulars, you know,' Max says bitterly.

I'm beginning to feel glad we'll be away soon for a few weeks.

Gina calls; she's looking for a bikini. Do I know where she can get one? This surprises me because although she is eager to learn to swim, all her lessons have to take place when it's dark. She is in the process of trying to lose weight and refuses to be seen in a swimming costume, especially by any of the hotel staff.

'We're putting on a show in the disco. Some of the army girls want to do it and since they're so far from home no one important will ever know about it and one of them needs a bikini.'

'Oh. I have a black bikini that I've hardly worn,' I offer, eager to help out.

'Could she borrow it?'

'OK,' I agree, hoping I can remember where I put it.

'This is great,' she says later when she comes to collect it. 'I'll let you have it back when the show is over.'

Rob is still away so we invite Judy to Gina's hotel for dinner on the night of the big show, which will be featuring, amongst other things, my bikini. She arrives dressed to the nines looking good in a red for danger lacy cocktail dress, which I know she has just had made for her. I am taken by surprise because it's only a casual meal but maybe she feels like dressing up.

We have our meal and go downstairs to the now-packed disco. Gina shows us to our seats beside the colonels and majors (I've lost track of who is what), orders our drinks and we wait for the action to happen. At this point a few scantily dressed young ladies arrive and Gina directs each one to sit on an officer's knee. We are sitting in the same line and as she finishes pointing to the colonel next to me, her finger drifts across in Mo's direction until my look penetrates her brain and her eyes catch mine. 'Wouldn't dare,' she says with her throaty laugh.

The lights dim and Gina, microphone in hand, introduces the show to the now-packed audience. It starts amidst a great deal of razzmatazz. It's supposed to be a kind of fashion show, and Mo, Judy and I are curious to see who's wearing my bikini. Coloured lights are flashing everywhere, and our eyes are busy scanning every female who dances in. I'm beginning to think it isn't going to make an appearance when a girl of colour appears wearing a black bikini.

'Is that yours?' Mo shouts (the noise is deafening).

'It must be,' I shout back, 'but I don't remember it looking like that. Do you?'

'Are you sure it's yours?' Mo frowns.

'Can't be that many black bikinis around. It has to be mine.'

'It looks good, she's got a really nice figure,' Judy shouts.

'Her boobs are bigger than mine. It looks a lot better on her,' I have to admit.

'She fills it out more,' says he who knows.

'Yeah,' I say dejectedly.

'Black isn't your colour anyway,' he says, giving me a playful nudge.

A little later Judy excuses herself. 'Just seen a friend,' she says. 'Excuse me, got to go and say hello.' She disappears.

Show over; we're about to leave. 'Any idea where Judy is?' I ask Gina.

'Oh, don't worry about her, she said she had seen a friend, she'll be OK.' This leaves me curious as to who the friend is.

The next time I see Judy, she tells me that the guy she met in the coffee shop was in town again and dropped in for a coffee at her house. It seems the colonel was watching, called Rob and told him he'd better get back ASAP. She's still furious. 'Who the hell does he think he is?' Her eyes narrow. 'Do you know I've discovered there's a hole in the fence where they can see through to our house? Their eyes must be permanently glued to the bloody thing. What did he think I was going to do with my daughter there, for heaven's sake?'

Thank God we chose the other house.

The news is that a big brawl occurred at one of the bars in town. No one told the GIs it was *Katoy* night.

Since Rob is now back, a crowd of us all go for a meal to the golf club. When the meal is over, rather than wait for the hotel minibus, Mo and Rob opt to run some people back home and as there isn't enough room for everyone in the cars, Judy and I decide we'll walk back to their house, as it isn't far from the golf club.

It's pitch-black, apart from the scant moonlight, and the road leading out of the golf club seems much longer than we remember. Finally, we reach the main road, and we still have a way to go. I'm beginning to wish we'd opted to wait at the clubhouse. We walk along the main road and just before we turn into the road leading to Judy's house, a couple of carloads of locals approach and slow down. They have obviously been drinking the local brew and seem to think we are imported hookers. This is more than a tad worrying because normally the Thai men aren't interested in us Western women.

We shoo them away and, heads held high, keep walking. Luckily, they're either too pissed or not that interested because eventually they drive off.

Now we turn into the road leading to Judy's house. I don't remember it being this long. To make matters worse it's toad season and tonight seems to be their equivalent to Woodstock because they are out in force. The noise, a loud bellowing that sounds like a herd of cows in agony, is haunting at the best of times. Now it sounds really loud and eerie on this dark, deserted road. As we hurry along, it seems to get louder, as do our footsteps. Everyone else is asleep and we wish we were; this is like something out of a horror movie. Finally, feeling decidedly shaken, we make it back. What a relief!

It's nearly time to go on leave and I am beginning to feel jittery about flying. Dan, who will be looking after things for Mo whilst we are on leave, is due to arrive in a few days' time, so Mo organises a room for him at the Pile Inn. We stay and have lunch, and one of the waitresses, a lovely girl called Lee, comes across to speak to us.

'Khun Dan is coming to stay in the hotel,' Mo tells her. 'Will you please be sure to look after him?'

'Yes, he'll be on his own, so please be really nice to him,' I add to emphasise our concern.

She laughs and gives us a big grin. 'Of course, Khun Mo, we take care, don worry.'

I put some cutlery, dishes and a coffee pot into a box for Dan since he will be here for a few weeks. He arrives with M and Mo takes them up to the hotel. He seems likeable and Mo is desperate for a break, so all should be well. Later we go out for dinner to a new restaurant by the riverside. It's built entirely of wood in the traditional Thai style and, being new, is the 'in' place to go, so it's also quite crowded, but nevertheless we have a great meal.

The book, which so far has only progressed in my mind, will have to be put on hold until we get back; I have too many distractions.

It's school holiday time and Khun Choochai and Khun Wipa set off to collect their sons and daughters from their respective schools up north. Whilst they are away the big gates, which are usually open during the day, are locked, and Mook and Sunti bugger off after lunch, no doubt to make the most of their employers' absence.

When the family are all back home again, they seem to spend all day inside and only come out in the late afternoon to swim and splash around in the pool.

The night before we are due to leave, Gina asks Judy, Beth and me to go up to the hotel to help entertain some of the air force people. When we get there, we discover it's actually a few of the officers she wants kept company. They are pilots and nice enough, but I get bored with the whole thing as the evening rolls on and then they decide they want to dance. Mo is in the pub, and I am getting increasingly fed up and don't really feel like dancing, so I make an excuse and phone him.

'Please come up to the hotel,' I plead with him. 'Gina's got us all dancing now with these guys and I've had enough.'

Luckily, he hasn't been drinking too much so is quite happy to come away. 'I'll be there soon,' he promises.

When he arrives a bit later, the dancing is abandoned, and we all sit down to have a drink. We mention that we are going home on leave and are due to fly tomorrow. One of them has a badge that another guy says means he is top gun. They are supposed to be going on exercises the next day and this guy is drinking like Prohibition is about to be announced. I'm wondering how he's going to think straight, never mind handle one of these supersonic jets or whatever it is they fly.

'Should you be drinking so much if you're going to be doing these exercises tomorrow, flying these jets?' I ask.

'What do you think the pilot who's flying your plane down to Bangkok tomorrow is doing now?'

'You mean he's drinking?'

'Course he is.'

'You're kidding me.'

'Nope.'

I stare at him in horror then realise my mouth is hanging open. I quickly clamp it shut.

'Now she won't sleep all night worrying,' Mo tells him.

'It's OK, these things fly themselves anyway,' he says. 'Have another drink.'

Bloody hell!

The night is long and the next morning we are up early to finish the last minute packing. Aroon drives us to the airport and as we are sitting waiting in the cafe, the girls arrive with flowers. This is totally unexpected, and we are very touched. It seems so strange to be leaving.

Despite my fears, we arrive safely in Bangkok and meet M for lunch. He takes us to a Japanese restaurant and, as always, orders for us. The food is wonderful. I wonder what it's going to be like, journeying back to our previous life.

Our first stop, San Francisco, is a whole world away from Thailand in every sense. We walk around outside and annoy car drivers by hovering at crossing signs unable to persuade ourselves that when we put a foot off the pavement we won't be run down.

In the evening we go for a meal, and I find myself talking slowly and carefully to the waiter in the Mexican restaurant as if he can't speak English. We snack on the freebie dips and tacos and then find it difficult to eat the actual meal when it comes. The next night Mo is really upset; he takes me to an upmarket restaurant as a treat. We both order fish. When the plates arrive, his is a tuna steak, mine is a huge fillet of swordfish. I can only manage a small bit of it. He's furious but there's nothing I can do. For a full year, my stomach has been accustomed to dishes with only bits of chicken, meat or fish. This is the real culture shock – going back.